D0522731

Nick Vandome

Dreamweaver CS5

in easy steps

WITHDRAWN

PRC LIBRARY

00077981

PETERBOROUGH LIBRARY REGIONAL COLLEGE

In easy steps is an imprint of In Easy Steps Limited
Southfield Road · Southam
Warwickshire CV47 0FB · United Kingdom
www.ineasysteps.com

Copyright © 2010 by In Easy Steps Limited. All rights reserved. No part
of this book may be reproduced or transmitted in any form or by any
means, electronic or mechanical, including photocopying, recording,
or by any information storage or retrieval system, without prior
written permission from the publisher.

Notice of Liability
Every effort has been made to ensure that this book contains accurate
and current information. However, In Easy Steps Limited and the
author shall not be liable for any loss or damage suffered by readers
as a result of any information contained herein.

Trademarks
Dreamweaver® is a registered trademark of Adobe Systems
Incorporated. All other trademarks are acknowledged as belonging to
their respective companies.

In Easy Steps Limited supports The Forest Stewardship Council (FSC),
the leading international forest certification organisation. All our titles
that are printed on Greenpeace approved FSC certified paper carry the
FSC logo.

MIX
Paper from
responsible sources
FSC® C020837

Printed and bound in the United Kingdom

ISBN 978-1-84078-407-7

Contents

PETERBOROUGH
REGIONAL COLLEGE
LIBRARY

006.7869

ACC.
No. 00077981

CLASS No. CHECKED

4/29/18

PETERBOROUGH LIBRARY REGIONAL COLLEGE

4 Working with Images   69

5 Using CSS   81

6 Formatting with CSS   105

7 Using Hyperlinks 125

8 Using Tables 133

9 Assets 143

10 Advanced Features 161

PETERBOROUGH
LIBRARY
REGIONAL COLLEGE

11 Publishing   177

Index   187

1 About Dreamweaver

Dreamweaver is a powerful web authoring tool that can be used to create highly professional websites. This chapter looks at the user interface of the program, and explains some of the features that will enable you to start working on creating web pages. These include the Insert panel, the Properties Inspector, and the Dreamweaver toolbars. It also shows how to use external editors for content.

Introducing Dreamweaver

In the early days of web design, the code used to create web pages was entered manually. This required the page designers to have a reasonable knowledge of the language, Hypertext Markup Language (HTML), in which it is written. While this is not a full-blown computer language, and it can be learned reasonably quickly, it can be a time-consuming business to create websites in this fashion.

The next development in web-design software was the introduction of HTML editors. These are programs that help make the process of creating HTML code quicker and easier, by giving the author shortcuts for adding the elements that make up the coded page. However, this still requires a good basic knowledge of HTML: it makes the process quicker for the experienced designer, but it does not help the novice much.

The big breakthrough in web-design software, and one that introduced a huge new audience to the joys of web design, was the introduction of WYSIWYG programs. WYSIWYG stands for 'What You See Is What You Get', and they enable people to design their own web pages without even having to be aware of the existence of HTML. They work in a similar way to a word-processing or a desktop-publishing program: what you lay out on the screen is what the end user will see on their computer. With these programs, the HTML is still present (and you can edit it manually if you desire) but it is all generated automatically by the program in the background.

Dreamweaver is primarily a WYSIWYG web authoring program that provides an effective interface for quickly creating high-quality web pages. In addition, it contains a range of powerful tools for incorporating the latest web-design elements into sites, to give them a highly professional look. Overall, Dreamweaver is an ideal program for anyone involved in designing websites: its combination of simplicity and power makes it an excellent choice for the novice and the professional alike. For the experienced web designer, Dreamweaver CS5 also has improved functions for using cascading style sheets (CSS), and extensions can also be obtained for using the latest version of HTML (5). These can be downloaded from the Adobe website, at www.adobe.com

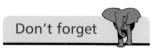

Don't forget

Before you start creating web pages, it is a good idea to learn the basics of HTML, either with a book or a course. There are numerous training courses and classes in HTML coding.

Don't forget

In 2005, Adobe completed the acquisition of Macromedia, the creators of Dreamweaver.

Don't forget

A new, advanced feature of Dreamweaver CS5 is support for working with Content Management Systems (CMS). However, this is aimed more at commerical web publishing and so is not covered in this book.

Start Screen

In order to help rationalize the number of options available when Dreamweaver is first opened, the latest version has a Start screen that appears initially, or when no other documents are open. The Start screen contains a variety of options for opening and creating documents, and also for obtaining help on using Dreamweaver CS5:

Click here to open a previously viewed file

Click here to create a new file

Check this box to disable the Start screen

Click here to access online help options for using the program

Don't forget

Even when you are using a WYSIWYG web authoring program, it is still important to follow the basics of good web design.

Hot tip

Click on the Top Features (videos) links to view short videos relating to some of the new features in CS5.

Workspaces

Within Dreamweaver CS5, there are a number of options for how you want to set up your work area, known as workspaces. These contain all of the main elements, but are arranged to suit how you want to work, mainly as a designer or a writer of code. To access and select different workspaces:

Don't forget

There are two other workspaces, named App Developer and App Developer Plus, that can be used by web developers using database technology and programming code.

1 Click here at the right-hand side of the main menu bar. Select the relevant workspace

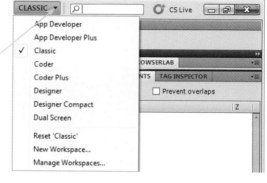

Classic

This is the workspace that was available with some earlier versions of Dreamweaver. By default, this displays toolbars, the main work area, and panels

One feature of the Classic workspace, is the location of the Insert panel, at the top of the main window, just below the menu bar.

Coder

This can be used if you mainly create web pages in code. The panels are arranged on the left-hand side and, by default, display those features most frequently used when working in code.

Don't forget

In the Coder workspace, it is still possible to access Design View to see how your page will look in a visual environment. For more information about the different views, see Chapter Two.

Coder Plus

This is an enhanced version of the Coder workspace, with additional panels situated on the right-hand side. The most notable of these is the Insert panel.

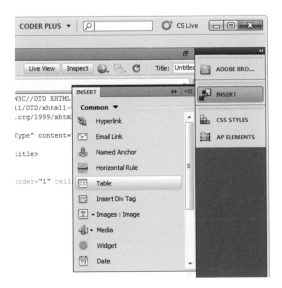

...cont'd

Designer

This is the default workspace, and is similar to the Classic workspace, except that the Insert panel is grouped with the rest of the other panels, at the right-hand side of the main window.

Don't forget

The styles and functionality of panels in Dreamweaver CS5 are now standardized with the panels in the other products in the CS5 suite of programs.

Designer Compact

This is similar to the standard Designer workspace, except that the panels are minimized, and group at the right-hand side. Each panel is activated by clicking on it, and it is then visible for one action. To keep a panel visible, drag it away from the group.

Workspaces (Mac)

With some previous version of Dreamweaver, the Mac version did not have the same versatility, in terms of workspaces. However, in CS5, this has been addressed, and the Mac version now has the same options as the Windows one. The only difference is the standard Mac interface:

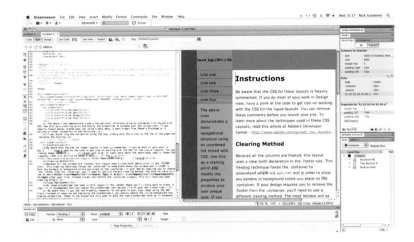

The same workspace options are available.

DESIGNER ▾   🔍

App Developer
App Developer Plus
Classic
Coder
Coder Plus
✓ Designer
Designer Compact
Dual Screen

Reset 'Designer'
New Workspace...
Manage Workspaces...

The same view options are also available (see Chapter Two).

| Code | Split | Design |

| Live Code | |

| Live View | Inspect |

Code
Split Code
Design
✓ Code and Design

✓ Split Vertically
Design View on Left

Preferences

Dreamweaver offers extensive options for the way the program looks and operates. These are located via the Preferences window. The preferences can be used to change the way the program and its elements appear, and also to change the way certain tasks are performed. There are 20 categories of preferences, and each category has several options. The Preferences options can be accessed by selecting Edit, Preferences (Windows) or Dreamweaver, Preferences (Mac), from the menu bar. Once the Preferences window has been accessed, it can be used to customize numerous elements of the program:

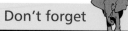

Don't forget

Take some time to look at the available preferences. Although you will not use all of them at this point, it is a good way to get a feel for the type of things you can change within the program.

1 Click here to select a category of preferences

Preferences

Category	General

General
Accessibility
AP Elements
Code Coloring
Code Format
Code Hints
Code Rewriting
Copy/Paste
CSS Styles
File Compare
File Types / Editors
Fonts
Highlighting
Invisible Elements
New Document
Preview in Browser
Site
Status Bar
Validator

Document options: ☑ Show Welcome Screen
☐ Reopen documents on startup
☑ Warn when opening read-only files
☑ Enable Related Files
Discover Dynamically-Related Files: Manually

Update links when moving files: Prompt

Editing options: ☑ Show dialog when inserting objects
☑ Enable double-byte inline input
☑ Switch to plain paragraph after heading
☐ Allow multiple consecutive spaces
☑ Use <strong> and <em> in place of <b> and <i>
☑ Warn when placing editable regions within <p> or <h1>-<h6> tags

Maximum number of history steps: 50

Spelling dictionary: English (United States)

Help   OK   Cancel

2 Select category options here, and click OK to apply them

Working with Panels

Panels in Dreamweaver CS5 contain numerous options for creating and editing content. They are docked along the side of the workspaces, to allow more space when designing pages. The panels can be selected from the Window menu on the menu bar. Once panels have been accessed, there are various ways in which to work with them.

1 Click and drag here to move a panel set

2 Click here to access a panel menu

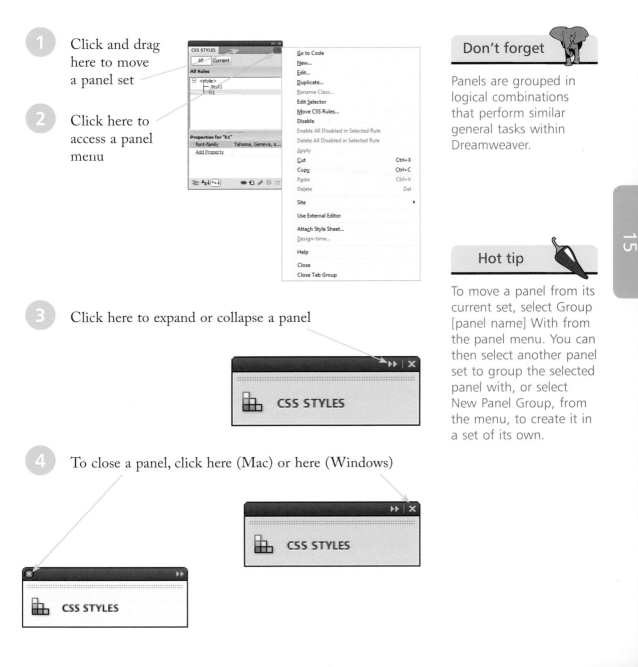

Don't forget

Panels are grouped in logical combinations that perform similar general tasks within Dreamweaver.

3 Click here to expand or collapse a panel

Hot tip

To move a panel from its current set, select Group [panel name] With from the panel menu. You can then select another panel set to group the selected panel with, or select New Panel Group, from the menu, to create it in a set of its own.

4 To close a panel, click here (Mac) or here (Windows)

15

Insert Panel

The Insert panel is the one that is used most frequently for adding content to web pages.

Common

This is the default setting, and the one that contains some of the most commonly used elements on a web page, such as hyperlinks, tables, images, and templates.

Layout

This provides options for creating tables, layers, and frames. It also provides various options for viewing tables.

Forms

This contains all of the elements that are used in online forms. For more information about this, see Chapter Ten.

Data

This contains buttons that can be used to insert data into the head section of a web page. This can include items, such as metadata, keywords, and descriptions. It also has options for adding scripts, such as Javascript, into an HTML document.

Spry

This contains buttons that can be used to insert Spry elements into a web page, for an improved experience for users. Spry elements are created with a combination of Javascript, cascading style sheets, and HTML, and include items like expanding menu bars and text-validation areas.

InContext Editing

This contains options for adding editable regions to pages.

Text

This contains buttons for inserting text functions, including bold, italics, preformatted text, headings, and lists. Some of these functions are also available on the Text Property Inspector, and also from the Text menu on the menu bar.

Favorites

This can be used to create a custom list of the most frequently used items within the Insert panel. To add Favorites, right-click (Ctrl+click on the Mac) on the Insert panel, and then select the required items in the Customize Favorites Objects window.

Don't forget

The Insert panel can be accessed by selecting Window, Insert, from the menu bar.

Don't forget

The head part of an HTML document contains information that is not displayed on the published page. One function of head information is to help search engines locate a page on the web.

Properties Inspector

The Properties Inspector displays the attributes of the currently selected item on the page, whether it is an image, a piece of text, a table, a frame, or an element of multimedia. In addition to viewing these attributes, you can alter them by entering values within the Properties Inspector. For instance, if you want to change the size of an image, you can select it, and then enter the new size required. To display the properties of a particular element, it has to be selected first.

Image properties

Select an image by clicking on it once, to display the relevant Properties Inspector:

Size   Dimensions   Location   Alt tag

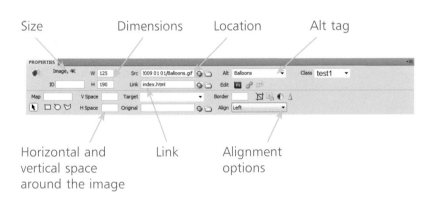

Horizontal and vertical space around the image   Link   Alignment options

Hot tip

When using images on a website, create a separate folder in which to store them. This way you will always know where the source for your images is.

HTML/CSS Toggle

Within the Properties Inspector, there are options for toggling between HTML options for adding specific tags, and CSS for formatting content. To toggle between the two:

1 Click on the HTML button to apply formatting tags, such as paragraph or heading tags

2 Click on the CSS button to add CSS rules, which can be used for items like text formatting

External Editors

When designing web pages, you will be working with a lot of elements that cannot be directly edited within Dreamweaver. These can include elements, such as sound files or movie clips, and images (although some editing can be done on images directly within Dreamweaver). One way to edit them would be to do so in an appropriate program, before they are inserted into Dreamweaver. However, if you then need to edit the items again, once they have been imported, it can be frustrating having to open up the file again, edit it, and then re-import it. Dreamweaver simplifies this process by providing direct links to external editors that can be used to edit items while they are still in the Dreamweaver environment.

It is possible to specify which program you want to use for specific tasks, e.g. editing images by selecting the file type and the program from the File Types / Editors category of the Preferences window:

Don't forget

The most commonly used external editors with Dreamweaver are for editing HTML code and editing images. HTML editing can be done with a text editor (such as Notepad on a PC or TextEdit on a Mac), and images can be edited with a graphics program, such as Fireworks or Photoshop.

 Select Edit, Preferences, from the menu bar, and select the File Types / Editors category

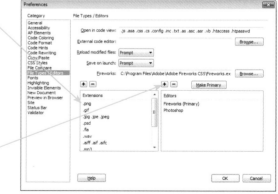

Click here to select a file type

Click here to select an external editor from your hard drive

Click OK

Using external editors

Once you have selected the required external editors for different file formats, it is then possible to access them while you are working on a page:

 Select an element on a page, such as an image

Beware

Files have to be saved and named before their content can be edited using an external editor. If you try and do this without saving a file, a dialog box will appear, asking you to save it.

19

Right-click (Windows) or Ctrl+click (Mac) on the item, and select the Edit With option that contains the primary editor for the selected item. To edit

| Reset Size |
| Reset Size To Original |
| Optimize... |
| Create Image |
| Edit With ▶ |
| Edit Original With ▶ |
| Add to Image Favorites |

the item with a different editor, select Edit With, and then browse to the program that you want to use to edit the selected item

To change the external editor for a specific file type at any time, select Edit, Edit with External Editor, from the menu bar, and change the selection in the File Types / Editors dialog box, as shown on the last page

Page Properties

In addition to setting preferences that affect all of the files you work on in Dreamweaver, it is possible to set properties for individual pages. These include items like background color, the color of links, and the margins on the page. To set page properties:

Don't forget

Hyperlinks, or just links, can be colored differently, depending on their current state. Different colors can be applied for a link before it has been activated, after it has been activated, and when it is in the state of being pressed.

Beware

If you are using a background image on a web page, make sure it is not too complex or gaudy. This could create a dramatic initial effect, but, if people are looking at the page a lot, it could become irritating. Similarly, background colors should, in general, be subtle and unobtrusive, rather than bright and bold. White is a very effective background for pages.

1 Select Modify, Page Properties, from the menu bar, or click on the Page Properties button on the Properties Inspector

2 Click here to select attributes for options, such as background images, text color, background color, and default page font

3 Click here to select other categories for the page properties. These include document title and tracing image (which is an image comprising a page design that can be inserted into a file and be used as the basis to create the actual page)

Page Tabs

Almost invariably, when a website is being created, a lot of different pages will be open at the same time. Keeping track of all of the open pages can be confusing, particularly if you are switching between different pages regularly. Dreamweaver CS5 has simplified this problem, by displaying all of the open pages in the form of tabs at the top of each page. This means that, provided your monitor is large enough, all of the open documents can be viewed and accessed at any time.

Click on a tab to move to that open document. This can be done with any open document

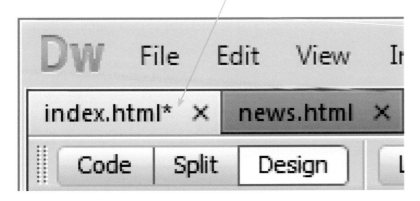

Hot tip

If an open file has an asterisk next to its name, this means that changes have been made but not yet saved. When the file is saved, the asterisk disappears.

21

For Dreamweaver on the Mac, pages are tabbed in the same way as for the Windows version, and files can also be closed by clicking on this icon for each individual file

Toolbars

Dreamweaver CS5 has a number of toolbars, which contain several options for specifying how the program operates. By default, these are displayed at the top of the page, although they can also be dragged to other locations. The toolbars can be accessed by selecting View, Toolbars, from the menu bar.

The two most commonly used toolbars are the Document toolbar, which contains the workspaces and views, and the Standard toolbar. The features of these include:

Document toolbar

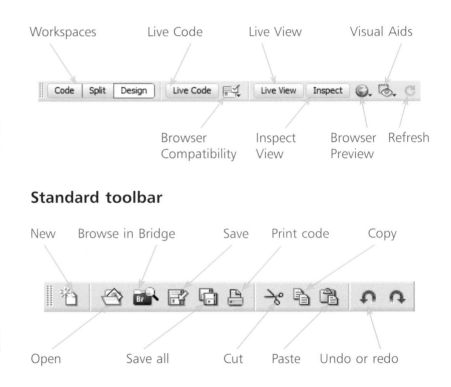

Standard toolbar

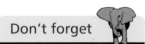

Don't forget

Another element of the Document toolbar is the Title box. This is where you enter the document title, which appears at the top of a web browser when a page is published online.

Don't forget

Browse in Bridge takes you to Adobe Bridge, which is a stand-alone program for browsing files, and looking for shared assets, particularly images, in other programs.

Don't forget

The other available toolbars are Style Rendering, for creating pages for different output devices, Coding, for working with code in Code view, and Browser Navigation, which is looked at in Chapter Two.

Using Guides

For some aspects of web design, considerable precision is required for positioning objects. This is particularly true when using style sheets (CSS) for formatting and layout purposes, where objects can be positioned at exact points on the page. To help with this, guides can be placed on the page, to position objects with pixel-precise accuracy. Guides are not visible when the completed web page is published. To use guides:

Don't forget

For a detailed look at CSS, and how to use them for formatting and layout purposes, see Chapters 5 and 6.

1 Select View, Guides, Show Guides, from the menu bar

2 Position the cursor over a horizontal or vertical ruler, and drag a guide onto the page

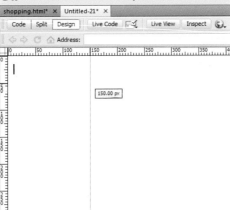

3 Hover over a guide on the page to see its exact location, in pixels

4 Guides can be used to create complex grids, which can then be used as a basis for the page content

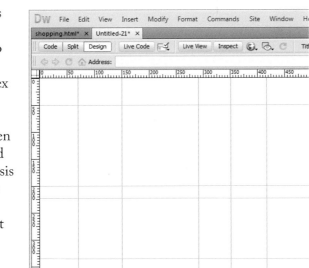

Hot tip

To view rulers on a page, select View, Rulers, Show, from the menu bar.

Accessibility

Accessibility options

An increasingly important issue for websites, and web designers, is the one of accessibility. This concerns the use of the Web by blind or partially sighted users. Despite the visual nature of the Web, this group of users can still access the information by using a technology that reads the content on screen. This means that someone who is blind, or partially sighted, is provided with an audio version of websites, rather than just a visual one.

Dreamweaver CS5 enables you to add accessibility features to web pages, as they are being created. To do this:

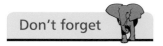

Don't forget

The accessibility guidelines used by Dreamweaver CS5 are based on those contained in Section 508 of the USA's 1998 Rehabilitation Act.

1   Select Edit, Preferences (Windows), Dreamweaver, Preferences (Mac) from the menu bar and click Accessibility

2   Check the items that you want to have accessibility features applied to

3   Click OK

Don't forget

Two websites to look at, for more information about accessibility issues, are the Section 508 site at www.section508.gov, and the Web Accessibility Initiative (WAI) at www. w3.org/wai.

4   Whenever one of the elements checked above is added to a web page, a dialog box appears where you can add in the appropriate accessibility features:

Checking accessibility

Dreamweaver no longer has its own accessibility checker, as it did in previous versions. However, there are websites that can be used to check the accessibility of your sites. One of these is WAVE, which can be accessed at http://wave.webaim.org/. To use this:

 Enter the web address (URL) into the web site address box, and click on the WAVE this page! button to check the site

Welcome to WAVE

WAVE is a free web accessibility evaluation tool provided by WebAIM. It is used to aid humans in the web accessibility evaluation process. Rather than providing a complex technical report, WAVE shows the original web page with embedded icons and indicators that reveal the accessibility of that page.

Enter a web site address

Enter the URL of the web site you want to evaluate.

Upload a file

If you have files that are not publicly available on the internet, you can upload the files for WAVE evaluation. Simply browse to the file using the form below.

Check HTML code

Paste HTML code into the text area below.

WAVE Blog

WAVE Downtime
April 29, 2010

WAVE Update
April 5, 2010

WAVE Dreamweaver Extension
January 30, 2010

WAVE User Survey
July 31, 2009

WAVE Update
July 28, 2009

Read more of the blog...

Browse to a file and enter it into the Upload a File box. Click on the WAVE this file! button, to check the file

Copy specific HTML code and paste it into the Check HTML Code box. Click on the WAVE this code! button to check the code

Getting Help

In common with most software programs, Dreamweaver offers an extensive range of help items. These include a general help index, online demonstrations of using the program, and websites for the latest upgrades.

Dreamweaver Help

The main help index is displayed in a browser window. This has a variety of options, all of which are accessed from the Help button on the menu bar:

Hot tip

The Help menu also has an option for registering your copy of Dreamweaver. This is done online, by connecting to the Adobe website. Once you have gone through the registration process, you will be able to get technical support for the product, and also receive the latest information about updates and upgrades.

1 Select Help, Dreamweaver Help, from the menu bar, and select a topic

2 The related item is opened in the online Adobe Community Help pages. Use the Search box to find items

Hot tip

The help files can be accessed by pressing F1 on the keyboard.

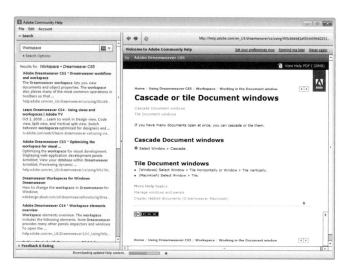

CS Live

In addition to the standard Dreamweaver Help, there is a new service that can be used for a variety of reference material and tutorials related to Dreamweaver, and for the other Adobe products in the CS5 suite. You have to have an Adobe ID to use CS Live, and then register for the service. This is subscription-based, but is available as a free trial until mid-2012. Once you have registered for CS Live, you can access it from Dreamweaver as follows:

1 Click on the CS Live button, at the top right corner of the Dreamweaver window

2 The available services are listed. Click on any of the items, or click on the Explore CS Live Services link

3 This takes you to the CS Live homepage

Hot tip

If you register a CS5 product before 30 April 2011, you can get 12 months complimentary access to CS Live services.

27

...cont'd

4 Enter 'Dreamweaver' in the Search box. The related resources are listed below the search box

Search: Dreamweaver

Adobe Dreamweaver
Buy now
Get help and support
Try now

Dreamweaver Developer Toolbox
Buy now
Get support
Try now

Dreamweaver Developer Center
Learn how to build websites that can grow and change with your needs.

Dreamweaver Developer: Get Started
Build skills with these tutorials, demos, and sample applications.

Dreamweaver Design Center
Find articles, tutorials, and instructional videos.

Dreamweaver community
Share knowledge, see what others are creating, and ask questions.

See all search results ›

Don't forget

CS Live also contains resources for other CS5 products, such as Photoshop, Flash, Illustrator, and Premier.

5 Click on an item to view the specific article or resource

2 Setting up a Site

This chapter looks at setting up a site structure, into which all of your page content will be placed. It also details the different layout views that can be deployed to diplay the design and code features in Dreamweaver.

PETERBOROUGH LIBRARY REGIONAL COLLEGE

Planning a Site

Websites that are published on the Internet are not just random pages thrown together in the hope that people will be able to view them over the Web. Instead, each site is a group of pages, images, and, if applicable, multimedia effects, linked together by a structure that is invariably created before any of the pages are created. It is possible to create web pages outside a web structure in Dreamweaver, and to store them on your own computer. However, when it comes to creating a whole site, it is important that you create a structure into which you can place all of the content for your site. When it comes to publishing your website on the Internet, you would encounter numerous problems if you had not already set up a site structure.

Preparing a structure

Before you start working with the site-structure tools in Dreamweaver, it is a good idea to decide where you want to store your sites, on your own hard drive. The pages, and other content for a website, are stored in a folder on your hard drive in exactly the same way as any other file. It is, therefore, a good idea to create a new folder for all of your web authoring files. As you create sites, you can create sub-folders from the main folder for each new site. Also, for each site, you may want to create sub-folders for all of the images and so on in your site. If you do this before you start creating your web pages, it will make it easier to save and add pages to a site. Once you have set up your folder structure, it could look something like this:

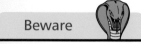

Beware

Do not create a new site in an existing folder that has other files in it. If you do, Dreamweaver will include all of these files in your site structure, even if they are not appropriate.

Hot tip

Draw a rough sketch of your proposed site structure before you start creating folders and files. This does not have to be the definitive structure, but it will give you a good overview of what you are trying to achieve.

◢ 📁 CS5 Website
   📁 _notes
  ▷ 📁 Content
   📁 CSS
   📁 Flash
  ▷ 📁 Images
  ▷ 📁 Library
   📁 Scripts
  ▷ 📁 SpryAssets
  ▷ 📁 Templates

Creating a New Site

After you have created a folder structure for your websites, you can begin to create individual sites within Dreamweaver. Once a site has been created, the content can then be added and built upon. If all of the items are stored within the same site structure, you will be able to perform a variety of site-management tasks with Dreamweaver. Within Dreamweaver CS5, there are options for setting up local and remote sites. The local site is the one on which you create files, and the remote site is where the completed pages and sites are published.

Local site definition

1 Select Site, Manage Sites, New, from the menu bar, and click the Site tab

2 Enter a name for the site

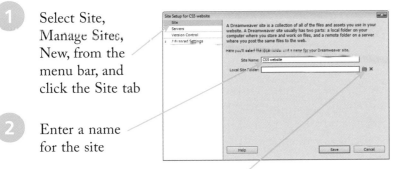

3 Click here to select a folder into which you can save your web files (the root folder)

4 Click on an existing folder, or create a new one, to serve as the root folder for your web files

31

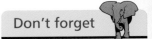

Don't forget

You can create as many structures for different websites as you like. But make sure each one has its own root folder.

Hot tip

Try and give your sites easily identifiable names, rather than just MySite or Website. If you are going to be creating a lot of websites, this is particularly important so that you can quickly identify which is which.

A message appears, saying that the cache will be created. This is a type of index that helps keep changes within the local site synchronized with the remote site. Click OK

 The new site is displayed in the Manage Sites window. Click on Done to exit the site setup

The new site is now listed in the Files panel. Files that are added to the site will appear here

Setting up the remote server

In a website structure, the remote server is the one where files are
published for viewing on the web. It is possible to create a website
without having a remote server, but they cannot be used on the
web until a remote server has been created with an Internet
Service Provider (ISP). To set up a remote server:

1 Access the Site Setup window, in the same way as for
creating a local site. Click on the Servers link, to access
the servers window

Don't forget

Checking files in and out
is used when a team is
working on a website,
and it is necessary to
be aware of which files
are being edited at any
one time. For more
information on this, see
Chapter 11.

33

2 Click here to add a new remote server

3 Click on the
Basic tab, and
then enter
the required
details.
These can be
acquired from
your Internet
Service
Provider (ISP)

Don't forget

FTP stands for File
Transfer Protocol and is
the standard method
for uploading files to a
remote server.

4 Click Save

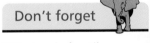

...cont'd

5 Click here to view the files located on the remote server. (These are only visible once they have been uploaded to the remote server)

Don't forget

A testing server is an area that can be used to preview how your site will look, and function, in an environment similar to the one to where you will publish the live site.

6 Click here to view the files located on the testing server (if being used)

Advanced Settings

Within the Site Setup window, there are a number of advanced settings that can be used to specify how your site operates. To use these settings:

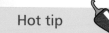
Hot tip

If you enable the cache, this will index the items within your site. This will help ensure that the files on your local site and your remote site will be synchronized.

1 In the Site Setup window, click on the Advanced Settings link. Click on Local Info to specify a default folder for images, and check on the Enable Cache box

2 Click on the Cloaking option to specify certain file types uploaded to the remote site by accident

3 Click on the Design Notes option to specify how you create, and share, information about your files, such as comments that are added to HTML or CSS pages

Site Setup for CS5 website
Site
Servers
Version Control
▼ Advanced Settings
Local Info
Cloaking
Design Notes

4 Click on the File View Columns option to specify how the Files panel operates, in terms of what is shown or hidden

Site Setup for CS5 website
Site
Servers
Version Control
▼ Advanced Settings
Local Info
Cloaking
Design Notes
File View Columns

Don't forget

Contribute is a complimentary program to Dreamweaver, it enables other users to update and publish their own pages within a website, without having to learn the full functionality of Dreamweaver.

5 Click on the Contribute option, if you are using this program to enable users to edit their own web pages and content

Site Setup for CS5 website
Site
Servers
Version Control
▼ Advanced Settings
Local Info
Cloaking
Design Notes
File View Columns
Contribute

35

6 Click on the Templates option to specify if you want certain file paths in templates to be updated, or not, when the template is edited

Site Setup for CS5 website
Site
Servers
Version Control
▼ Advanced Settings
Local Info
Cloaking
Design Notes
File View Columns
Contribute
Templates

Don't forget

Spry elements are Javascript items that can add increased functionality to websites. For more information on this, see Chapter Ten.

7 Click on the Spry option to specify a folder for storing Spry elements, if you are using them

Site Setup for CS5 website
Site
Servers
Version Control
▼ Advanced Settings
Local Info
Cloaking
Design Notes
File View Columns
Contribute
Templates
Spry

Creating Pages

When creating new pages, after File, New is selected from the menu bar, Dreamweaver CS5 offers considerable flexibility. You may, if you wish, create a blank page (with no formatting or pre-inserted elements) by selecting Blank Page, HTML, but there are a lot more options available to you:

1 Select File, New, from the menu bar

2 Click on the Blank Page tab

Don't forget

By default, basic HTML pages are created as XHTML files. This is a version of HTML that enables documents to be used in an XML environment, if required. The default document type can be set in the New Document category of the Dreamweaver Preferences, and it is worth keeping this as XHTML, as it will give the file a certain degree of future-proofing.

3 Select the type of document you want to create

4 Click Create

Page-design templates

One of the options, when creating new pages, is to use one of the page designs that have already been stored within Dreamweaver CS5. This can be a good way to quickly create the basis of professionally designed Web pages. To use page-design templates:

1 Select File, New, from the menu bar

2 Click on the Blank Page tab

3 Select a Page Type, and the design you want to use

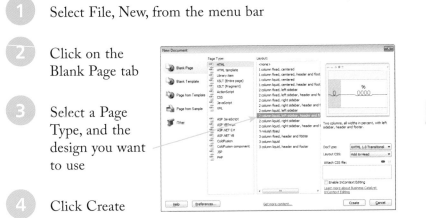

4 Click Create

5 A new document is created, based on the page design selected above

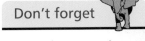

Don't forget

Once a document has been created, based on a page design, the content can be customized to meet your own requirements.

37

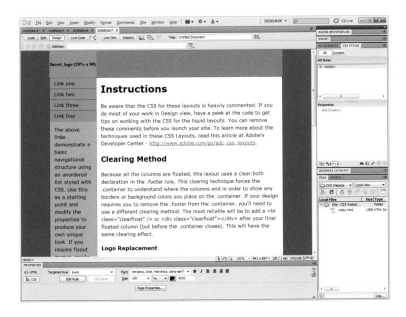

Layout Views

In addition to the workspace options shown in Chapter One, there are also several ways that the content in each workspace can be viewed. These can be accessed from the Document toolbar:

They can also be selected from the menu bar by clicking on the Layout button. (This can also be used to determine the position of Design View, if it is being used in conjunction with Code View.)

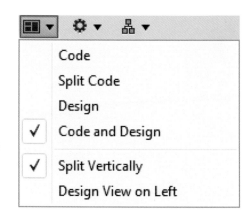

Hot tip

By default, Design View is located on the right, if it is being used with Split View. This can be changed by selecting the Design View on Left option, from the Layout button on the menu bar.

38

Design View

This is the What You See Is What You Get (WYSIWYG) view. The content is laid out graphically on the page, and this is generally how it will appear in a web browser.

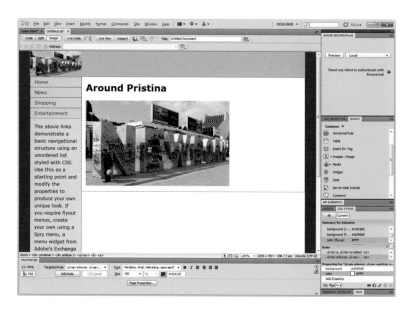

Code View

This view displays the code of the web page. If you are working in this view, you should have a working knowledge of HTML and also CSS.

Don't forget

You can switch between the different views at any time, to check the code or design, as required.

Split View

In some ways the best of both worlds, Split View displays two windows, one with code and the other with design (although both have a more limited size of display than with their own individual views.) As with the individual views, when a change is made in one area, this is also applied in the other view.

Hot tip

If you are using Split View, and make changes in the code, click on the Refresh button to apply the changes to the Design View.

Live View

An innovation in recent versions of Dreamweaver, including CS5, is Live View. This enables you to view the functionality of your web page without leaving Dreamweaver, i.e. you do not have to preview it in a web browser. With the increasing use of items, such as Javascript driven menus, video, and other dynamic element, Live View is a great way to see how your creations will operate. To access Live View, click on the Live View button on the Document toolbar:

1 The page is displayed as it will be rendered in a web browser. Content cannot be edited in Live View

2 Move the cursor over elements to see how they react

3 Functionality will be displayed, such as for rollover menus

4 Links and navigation can also be checked in Live View. To do this, Ctrl+click (Windows) on a link, or Cmd+click (Mac)

5 The linked page opens in Live View

Hot tip

Live View can be exited by clicking on the Live View button again.

6 Use the navigation on this page to move to other linked page, and to preview them in Live View too

Live View Navigation

Because of the power and versatility of Live View, you can sometime start to feel a bit lost if you are moving between numerous pages. To help combat this, there is a Browser Navigation toolbar to help. This works in a similar way to a standard web browser toolbar: you can navigate between pages you have visited, set a homepage, and it shows the address of the page you are currently viewing. To use the Browser Navigation toolbar:

1   If the Browser Navigation toolbar is not showing, select View, Toolbars, Browser Navigation, from the menu bar

2   The Browser Navigation toolbar is located directly underneath the Document toolbar

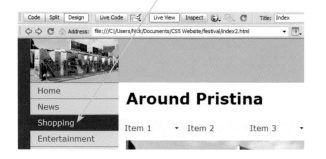

3   In Live View, use a link to navigate to another page

Don't forget

The Browser Navigation bar has a homepage button. This is the page you start from each time you start a new session using the Browser Navigation bar.

4   Click on the Back button to move to the previous page

Live Code

Live Code is a view that gives added functionality to Live View. It enables elements to be highlighted in Live View, and then the relevant code is highlighted in Live Code. It is also possible to edit the code. When Live Code is accessed, Live View is also activated automatically. To use Live Code:

1 Click on the Live Code button on the Document toolbar

2 In Live Code, the code area is colored yellow, next to the Live View window

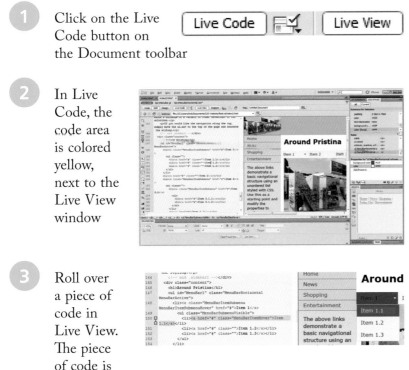

3 Roll over a piece of code in Live View. The piece of code is highlighted in Code View

4 Press F6 to freeze the code. Changes can be made using elements, such as the CSS Styles panel. These changes can be viewed in the Live View window

Don't forget

For more information about add, creating, and editing CSS, see Chapters Five and Six.

Related Files

Web pages have come a long way since single, static HTML files. They are now feature-rich, and one HTML page can be linked to several other types of files: CSS files for formatting and styling, and javascript files for functionality, such as video. In Dreamweaver, it is not only possible to view files that are related to the one you are working, you can also amend the related files, and see the effect this has on your source file. To view and use related files:

1 When a file is opened, it is displayed in one of the workspaces, where design and code can be viewed

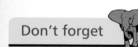

Don't forget

Related files are shown, regardless of which View you are working in.

2 By default, the source code for the file is displayed in Code View

3 The Source Code button is highlighted under the file name. Any other related files are displayed next to the Source Code button

wildlife.html* ✕

Source Code   wildlife_css.css   swfobject_modified.js

4 Click on another button to view the code for the related file, the code for the CSS file in this example

Don't forget

If you are working in Design View, and click on a related file, this will activate Code View, and the related file will be shown here.

45

5 The code for different file types can be viewed, the code for a Javascript file that is used to display video in this example

Don't forget

If changes are made in a related file, these are applied to the source file, once the related file has been saved.

6 Click on the buttons underneath the filename, to view that related file. Click back on the Source Code button to return to the original Source Code

wildlife.html ✕

Source Code   wildlife_css.css*   swfobject_modified.js

Moving Around Pages

Because of the power and sophistication of Dreamweaver, page designs can quickly become very involved and complex. Because of this, it is useful to be able to move around pages, and also to zoom in to specific sections to see the design in close-up. This can help you create pages as accurately as possible. To do this:

Don't forget

Use the Hand tool to move around a page, by clicking within the page and dragging around different parts of it.

1 Open a file. By default, this will be displayed at 1:1 size, i.e. 100%

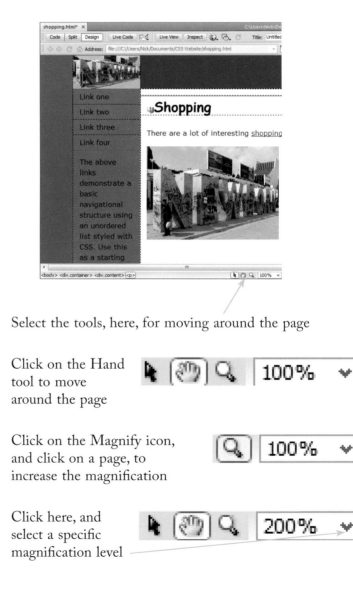

Hot tip

To decrease magnification, hold down Alt, click on the Zoom tool (magnifying glass), and click on the page.

2 Select the tools, here, for moving around the page

3 Click on the Hand tool to move around the page   100% ✔

4 Click on the Magnify icon, and click on a page, to increase the magnification   100% ✔

5 Click here, and select a specific magnification level   200% ✔

3 Editing HTML

This chapter looks at the options Dreamweaver provides for adding and editing HTML (Hypertext Markup Language) code, which is used to create web pages. It shows how to create your own code, and covers some of the features that assist in the process and help to speed it up.

HTML Overview

Hypertext Markup Language (HTML) is the computer code used to create web pages. It is not a fully-blown computer-programming language, but is rather a set of instructions that enables a web browser to determine the layout of pages.

HTML is created by using a series of tags, which contain the instructions that are interpreted by the browsers. These tags are placed around the item you want that particular command to apply to. Most tags, but not all of them, have an opening and a closing element. The opening tag contains the particular command, and the closing tag contains the same command, but with a "/" in front of it, to denote the end of the command. For instance, if you wanted to display a piece of text as bold, you could do it with the following piece of HTML:

<strong>This text would appear bold in a browser</strong>

HTML is a text-based code, which means that the source HTML file only contains text, and not any images or multimedia items. These appear in the browser because of a reference to them placed in an HTML document. For instance, if you wanted to include an image in a document, you would insert the following piece of HTML into your source file:

<img src="myimage.jpg">

This would instruct the browser to insert this image at the required point within the HTML document, when it is being viewed on the Web. It is possible to insert HTML code to call for a variety of graphics and multimedia files to be displayed in a web page. However, it is important to remember that when you are publishing your pages, all of the items that are referred to in the source HTML document are uploaded to the server, as well as the HTML file.

Since Dreamweaver is a "what you see is what you get" (WYSIWYG) program, it generates all of the HTML in the background. This means that it is possible to ignore the HTML's existence completely. However, it is useful to learn the basics.

Don't forget

Increasingly, cascading style sheets (CSS) are used to format content within HTML files. For more information on this, see Chapters Five and Six.

Don't forget

For more detailed information about HTML, take a look at "HTML in Easy Steps".

Hot tip

Previously, <b> and <i> tags have been used for creating bold and italics, respectively, in HTML code. However, these have now generally been replaced with the <strong> and <em> tags. This is primarily for accessibility reasons, to make it easier for page readers to add emphasis to web pages.

Common tags

Unless otherwise stated, tags have an equivalent closing tag, created by inserting "/" in front of the command. Some of the most commonly used tags in HTML are:

- <p>   This creates a new paragraph

- <strong>   This creates bold text

- <em>   This creates italics

-
   This inserts a line break (this does not have a closing tag)

- <hr>   This inserts a horizontal line (this does not have a closing tag)

- <img src="image.jpg">   This inserts the specified image (this does not have a closing tag)

- <font face="Arial">   This was how text was formated, when the formatting was done in the HTML code. It can still be used on web pages, but it is now best practice to create the formatting in the CSS code. The font tag is now known as a deprecated tag, i.e. one that is no longer used. The closing tag is just </font>

- <h1>   This formats text at a preset heading size. There are six levels for this, "h1" being the largest and "h6" being the smallest. Paragraph and other formatting tags cannot be used within heading tags

- <table>   This inserts a table

- <color="ffffff">   This can be used to select a color for a variety of items, including background color and text color. This is another tag that is now more frequently done in the CSS code

- <a href="default.htm">Home Page</a>   This is used to create a hyperlink to another web page. In this case, the link is to the file "default.htm" and the words "Home Page" will appear underlined on the web page, denoting that it is a link to another page

Page Views

Although it is possible to be blissfully unaware of the existence of HTML when you are using Dreamweaver, you can also hand-code pages using Code view. This allows you to create your own HTML code, which is then translated into the document window, by Dreamweaver. This can be a good way to learn about HTML, and to perform fine-tuning tasks if you cannot achieve the result you want through the document window. In Dreamweaver CS5, you can access the graphical version of the page, the HTML code on its own, or a combination of them both:

Don't forget

When Code View and Design View are showing together, if any changes are made in one of these views, the other is updated automatically.

Click here to access Code and Design View together

Click here to access Design View on its own

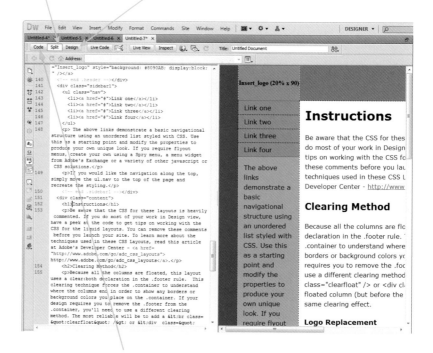

Click here to access the Code View on its own

HTML Preferences

Code colors

When creating and editing HTML within Dreamweaver, it is possible to set various defaults for the colors within the HTML Source window. This can be useful, not only for aesthetic reasons, but also to make specific elements stand out within the code. These elements can then be quickly identified when working with the source code. To set the preferences for colors within the HTML Source window:

1 Select Edit, Preferences, from the menu bar

2 Select Code Coloring in the Preferences dialog box

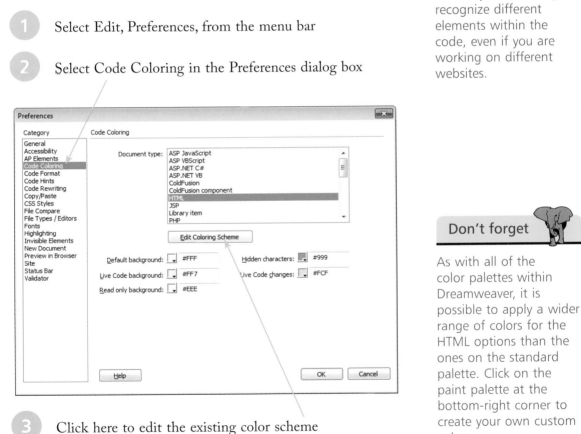

3 Click here to edit the existing color scheme

4 Click OK

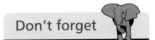

Don't forget

Use a consistent theme for colors within the HTML Source window, so that you can easily recognize different elements within the code, even if you are working on different websites.

Don't forget

As with all of the color palettes within Dreamweaver, it is possible to apply a wider range of colors for the HTML options than the ones on the standard palette. Click on the paint palette at the bottom-right corner to create your own custom colors.

...cont'd

The options for setting colors for code coloring are:

- Background. This affects the background color of the window

- Text. This affects the color of the text that appears in the document

- Bold, italic and underlining

Hot tip

One of the most versatile ways of aligning and laying out images and text is through the use of tables. This will enable you to produce precision alignment. The alignment options on this page can also be applied to images and text, once they are inserted into a table. For more on tables, see Chapter Eight.

Select a tag from this list

Click here to select a font color

Edit Coloring Scheme for HTML

Styles for:

HTML Special Characters
HTML Style Tags
HTML Table Tags
HTML tags
HTML Text
JavaScript Bracket
JavaScript Client Keywords
JavaScript Comment
JavaScript Default Text
JavaScript Function Keyword
JavaScript Identifier
JavaScript Native Keywords

Text color: #000

Background color: #FFF

B *I* <u>U</u>

OK

Cancel

Preview:

```
<style> headline {font-size: 24pt;} </style>
<!-- Comment -->
<td><p><a href="link">Plain Text </a>
<img src="image" width=15 />
<script>
<!--
    function testMe() {
        var i = abs(-134) + "test";
```

Help

Apply formatting to the color scheme

Preview the color scheme here

Code formats

These preferences can be used to determine the layout of the code within the HTML Source window. These include the way tags are presented, and also the use of indents and tabs to indicate certain elements, such as tables and frames. To access the Code Format preferences:

Select Code Format from the Preferences dialog box

Click here to specify how indents are displayed and which items will appear indented

Enter tab values

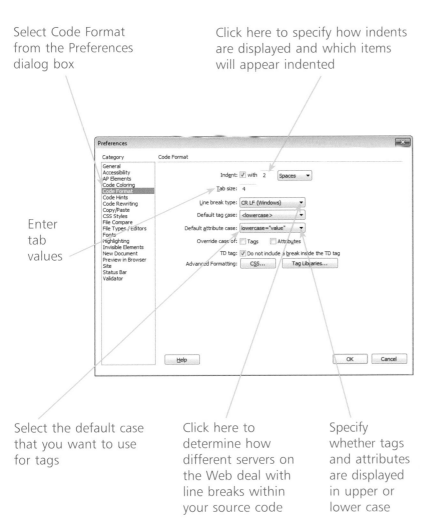

Select the default case that you want to use for tags

Click here to determine how different servers on the Web deal with line breaks within your source code

Specify whether tags and attributes are displayed in upper or lower case

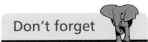

Don't forget

According to the values that are set, different elements on a page will be displayed with code that is indented in the HTML source. For instance, the code for table rows, columns and frames, is usually indented.

Beware

Before you start creating web pages, decide whether you want your tags to be in upper or lower case. Once you have done this, stick to it for all of your pages and sites, for the sake of consistency. In general, lower-case tags are neater and take up less space in the code.

53

Coding Toolbar

In Code view, there is a toolbar to help with entering and editing HTML code. The elements of this are:

Hot tip

If the Coding toolbar is not visible in Code View, select View, Toolbars, Coding, from the menu bar.

Hot tip

The Balance Braces option can be used to check that every opening tag has the corresponding closing tag, if required.

Don't forget

Comments are elements that are only visible in the code, and they can be used as reminders to insert a particular item, or to specify exactly what is contained within the code. They can be used to make (hidden) personal comments in the code of a file.

Code Navigator

Open documents (displays currently open files)

Collapse full tag

Collapse selection

Expand all

Select parent tag

Balance braces

Show or hide line numbers

Highlight invalid code

Word Wrap

Syntax Errors

Apply comment

Remove comment

Wrap tag

Recent snippets

Move or convert CSS

Indent code

Outdent code

Format source code

Collapsing Code

When working in Code view, it is sometimes useful to be able to collapse sections of code, so that work can be done on other elements of the code. There are various ways in which this can be done within Code view:

1 Click here, on the Coding toolbar, to display line numbers next to the code

2 Select a tag in the code, and click next to the line number to select the whole tag

3 Click on the minus sign to collapse the code

4 Click on the plus sign to expand the code

6 Use the Code toolbar to expand and collapse selections:

Collapse the whole of a selected tag

Collapse selected code

Expand all of the code

Select the parent tag of a selection

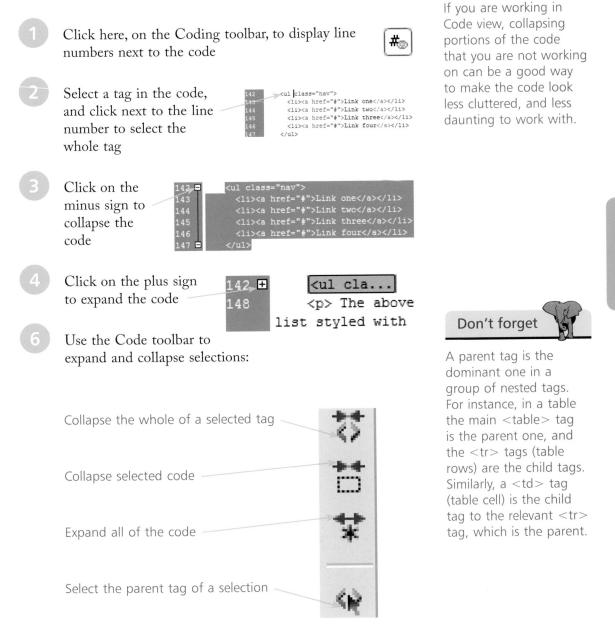

Hot tip

If you are working in Code view, collapsing portions of the code that you are not working on can be a good way to make the code look less cluttered, and less daunting to work with.

Don't forget

A parent tag is the dominant one in a group of nested tags. For instance, in a table the main <table> tag is the parent one, and the <tr> tags (table rows) are the child tags. Similarly, a <td> tag (table cell) is the child tag to the relevant <tr> tag, which is the parent.

Tag Chooser

To speed up the process of creating HTML, Dreamweaver has a number of functions for inserting HTML tags, or blocks of code, rather than having to create it all by hand. One of these is the Tag Chooser, where HTML tags can be inserted with a couple of mouse clicks. To do this:

Hot tip

Once the Insert button is clicked on, in the Tag Chooser dialog box, the selected tag is entered into Code view, but the dialog box remains visible until Close is clicked. Therefore, keep the Code view window visible, so that you can see when the code has been added. This means that you can add several tags without having to activate the Tag Chooser dialog box each time.

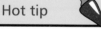

Hot tip

Some tags have additional properties that can be added in a dialog box, once the tag has been selected.

1 Insert the cursor in Code view, at the point where you want the tag to appear

```
151     <div class="content">
152         <h1>Instructions</h1>
153     
154         <p>Be aware that the
```

2 Right-click (Windows) or Ctrl+click (Mac) and select Insert Tag

3 In the Tag Chooser window, select the tag you want to use, and click Insert

4 The tag is inserted into the document at the insertion point

```
152     <h1>Instructions</h1>
153     <hr align="center" width="80%" />
154     <p>Be aware that the CSS for these
```

Tag Libraries

The tags that appear in the Tag Chooser are stored in the Tag Library. It is possible to add tags to the Tag Library, and also to edit existing ones. This gives increased versatility for the HTML tags at your disposal. To edit tags in the Tag Library:

1 Select Edit, Tag Libraries, from the menu bar

2 Select a tag to view its attributes, and edit them as required

3 Click here to create a new library for your own tags, or to create new tags. Click OK

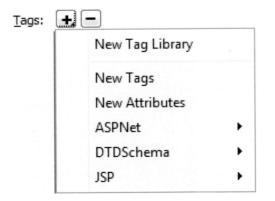

Hot tip

You may want to create new Tag Libraries and tags, if you are using a server technology, such as Active Server Pages or ColdFusion.

4 For a new Tag Library, click on the New Tag Library link

Tag Inspector

The Tag Inspector is a panel that enables you to see the attributes for a selected item, and to amend them, if required. To use the Tag Inspector:

 Select an item to view its properties in the Tag Inspector

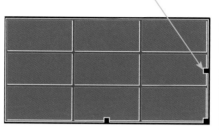

Don't forget

The number of attributes shown in the Tag Inspector depends on the item selected: there will be more for some items than for others.

2 Select an attribute, and enter details here to change its parameters

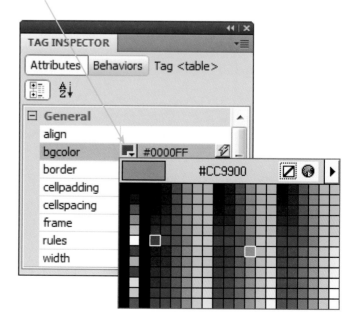

3 The changes in the Tag Inspector will be applied to the selected object

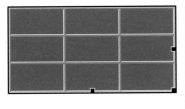

4 Click here and select Edit Tag

5 Enter new parameters for the tag in the Tag Editor

Beware

Once a change has been made to a tag in the Tag Editor, this only applies to the selected item. It does not apply to any similar items that are subsequently created.

59

6 Click here to view reference information about the selected tag

7 Click OK

Code Snippets

One of the new features of Dreamweaver CS5 is the ability to add blocks, or snippets, of HTML code into documents. This is done with the Snippets panel, and existing snippets can be used, as well as creating new ones. To use the Snippets panel:

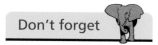

Don't forget

Code snippets are grouped in folders containing similar types of snippets. However, it is possible to move snippets, and also folders, by dragging and dropping them to another folder.

1 Click the Snippets tab to view the current Snippets folders

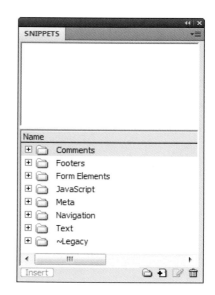

Don't forget

Even though their name suggests otherwise, code snippets can include some lengthy elements of HTML code.

2 Select a folder by double-clicking on it, and select a snippet within it by clicking on it once

3 Click Insert

4 The selected snippet of code is inserted into the current document. Depending on the type of snippet, it will be displayed in Design view and Code view. However, some snippets, such as metadata, will only be displayed in Code view

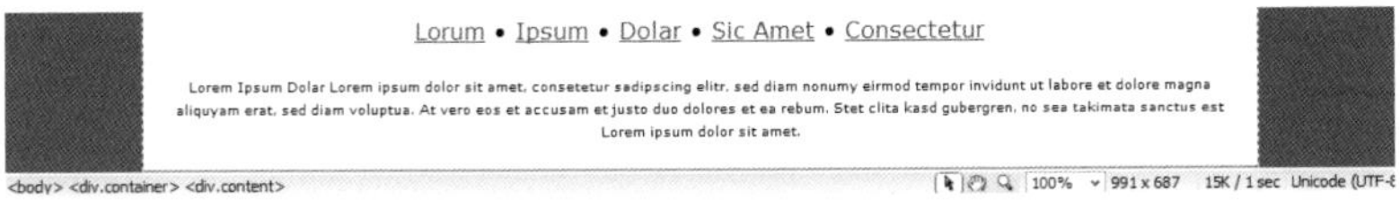

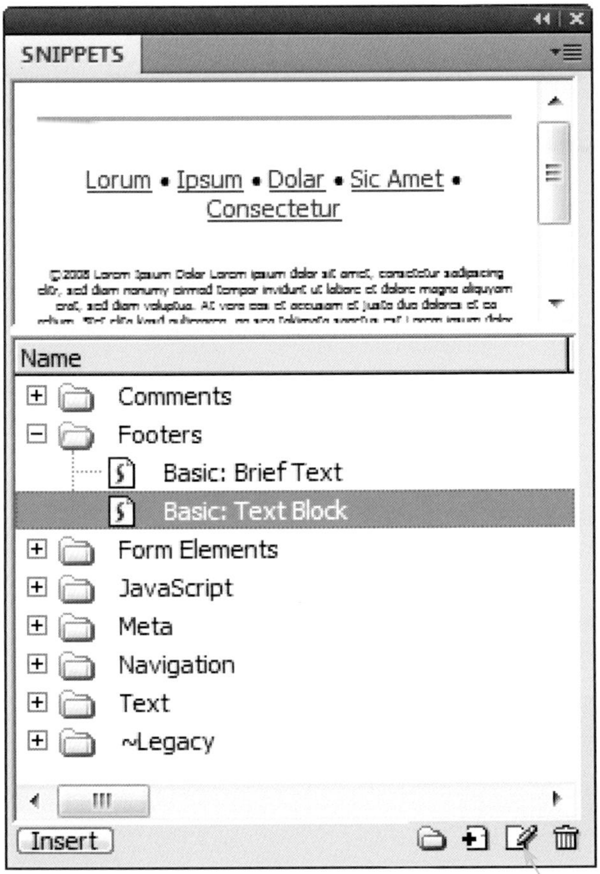

Don't forget

Metadata are contained within the <head> tag of an HTML page, and they store items, such as keywords and descriptions about a page, which can be used by search engines trying to locate the page. Metadata can also include other items, such as information about how frequently a page should be automatically refreshed by the browser, if required.

Lorum • Ipsum • Dolar • Sic Amet • Consectetur

Lorem Ipsum Dolar Lorem ipsum dolor sit amet, consetetur sadipscing elitr, sed diam nonumy eirmod tempor invidunt ut labore et dolore magna aliquyam erat, sed diam voluptua. At vero eos et accusam et justo duo dolores et ea rebum. Stet clita kasd gubergren, no sea takimata sanctus est Lorem ipsum dolor sit amet.

`<body> <div.container> <div.content>`   100% ∨ 991 x 687   15K / 1 sec   Unicode (UTF-8

SNIPPETS

Lorum • Ipsum • Dolar • Sic Amet • Consectetur

©2008 Lorem Ipsum Dolar Lorem ipsum dolor sit amet, consectetur sadipscing elitr, sed diam nonumy eirmod tempor invidunt ut labore et dolore magna aliquyam erat, sed diam voluptua. At vero eos et accusam et justo duo dolores et ea rebum. Stet clita kasd gubergren, no sea takimata sanctus est Lorem ipsum dolor

Name
⊞ 📁 Comments
⊟ 📁 Footers
⌐ �$ Basic: Brief Text
�$ Basic: Text Block
⊞ 📁 Form Elements
⊞ 📁 JavaScript
⊞ 📁 Meta
⊞ 📁 Navigation
⊞ 📁 Text
⊞ 📁 ~Legacy

[Insert]   📁 📥 📝 🗑

5 To edit an existing snippet, select it in the Snippets panel, and click here

...cont'd

6 The code that makes up the snippet is displayed in the Snippet dialog box

Hot tip

One very useful snippet can be found in the Navigation folder, in the Snippets panel. It is the Breadcrumbs snippet, and it can be used at the top of a page to denote exactly where the user has reached within a site.

Snippet	
Name: Basic: Text Block	OK
Description: A bullet-separated list of links, with detailed information below.	Cancel
	Help
Snippet type: ○ Wrap selection ⦿ Insert block	

Insert code:
```
<div style="text-align: center; border-top: 2px solid #999; mar
<p><a href="#">Lorum</a> • <a href="#">Ipsum</a> • <a
<p style="font-size: 0.6em;"> Lorem Ipsum Dolar Lorem ipsum d

          sadipscing elitr, sed diam nonumy eirmod tempor invidunt u

          dolore magna aliquyam erat, sed diam voluptua. At vero ec

          et justo duo dolores et ea rebum. Stet clita kasd gubergren

          sanctus est Lorem ipsum dolor sit amet.</p>
</div>
```

Preview type: ⦿ Design   ○ Code

7 Make any changes that are required, and click OK

Creating new snippets

Don't forget

Any piece of code that you think you will use frequently should be saved as a snippet.

1 Select an item on a page

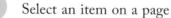

2 In the Snippets panel, select a folder into which you want to include the snippet

3 Click here, and select New Snippet

SNIPPETS

Name
⊞ 📁 Comments
⊞ 📁 Footers
⊞ 📁 Form Elements
⊞ 📁 JavaScript
⊞ 📁 Meta
⊞ 📁 Navigation
⊞ 📁 Text
⊞ 📁 ~Legacy

Insert

4 The code for the snippet is already inserted. Enter a name and description for the snippet, and, if necessary, amend the code

Snippet

Name: Table (purple)

Description:

Snippet type: ● Wrap selection   ○ Insert block

Insert before:
```
<table width="400" height="141" border="1" align="left" cellpa
  <tr>
    <td bgcolor="#9966CC"> </td>
    <td bgcolor="#9966CC"> </td>
    <td bgcolor="#9966CC"> </td>
  </tr>
  <tr>
    <td bgcolor="#9966CC"> </td>
    <td bgcolor="#9966CC"> </td>
```

Insert after:

Preview type: ● Design   ○ Code

OK   Cancel   Help

6 Click OK

7 The new snippet is added to the new folder in the Snippets panel, and can now be used in the same way as any other snippet

Hot tip

The HTML code for inserting an image can be created as a snippet, in the same way as any other piece of HTML code: select an image and select New Snippet from the Snippets panel menu to add the code.

63

Don't forget

The preview type can be set to Design or Code. This determines how the snippet is displayed, in the Preview panel of the Snippets panel. Design gives a graphical preview, and Code displays the HTML code.

Invalid Code

If you write any invalid code in the Code view, or turn off all of the HTML Rewriting preferences when opening a document from another source, any invalid code will be highlighted in yellow, in both the Code-view window and the Design-view window. This means that Dreamweaver has encountered some code that it does not understand, and, therefore, it cannot display it correctly or reformat it automatically. However, it is possible to manually correct any invalid code:

1   Click on the tags that denote invalid HTML code. This can be done either in the Code View window or in Design View. An invalid code tag is colored yellow

2   A window will appear, alerting you to the reasons for the invalid code, and instructing you how to repair it. Follow these instructions and check that the invalid code tags have subsequently disappeared

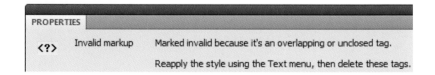

Don't forget

On occasions, a whole string of HTML tags will be marked as being invalid. However, this can sometimes be corrected by fixing one tag, by changing its nesting order for example.

Hot tip

If you are familiar with HTML, it can be quicker to fix invalid code in the Code View window than in Design View.

Don't forget

If you encounter any invalid code on your pages, press F12 to see how this affects the page when it is viewed in a browser. In some cases, it will be unnoticeable.

Quick Tag Editor

When editing HTML code, there will probably be times when you want to quickly change or add a specific tag. This can be done by accessing Code view. However, it is also possible to do this without leaving Design view, through the use of the Quick Tag Editor. This is a function that enables you to insert and check HTML tags directly in the Design-view window. Any changes that are made are updated automatically in the Code-view window. The Quick Tag Editor can be accessed by selecting Modify, Quick Tag Editor from the menu bar, or by using Ctrl+T (Windows) or Command+T (Mac). This shortcut can also be used to toggle between the different modes of the Quick Tag Editor.

There are two different modes that can be used within the Quick Tag Editor:

Insert HTML mode

This enables you to insert new HTML tags into a document. If required, it can be used to insert a string of several tags together. If the closing tags are not inserted, then Dreamweaver will automatically place these in the most appropriate place.

1. Insert the cursor at the point where you want to create a new HTML tag. Do not select any elements on the page

2. Press Ctrl+T (Windows) or Command+T (Mac) and enter the required tag and any content. If you wait a couple of seconds, a drop-down hints menu will appear with a choice of tags to use

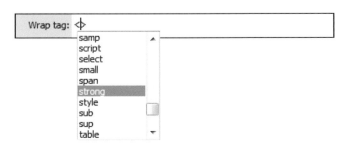

65

Beware

When inserting tags with the Quick Tag Editor, it is best to insert the corresponding closing tag at the required point as well. Check in the HTML Source window to make sure that the tags have been inserted in the correct places.

Don't forget

Insert HTML mode can be used to insert both opening and closing tags, and also the content between them.

Don't forget

Once tags have been entered in the Quick Tag Editor, the changes can be applied by clicking back in Design View.

...cont'd

Edit Tag mode

This can be used to edit existing HTML tags in a document. The Quick Tag Editor opens in this mode, if an item with an opening and closing tag is selected on the page.

1 Select an element on the page that contains an opening tag, content, and a closing tag. This could mean selecting an image, or an entire section of formatted text

2 Press Ctrl+T (Windows) or Command+T (Mac) to open the Quick Tag Editor in Edit Tag mode

```
Edit tag: <img src="images/pristina2.jpg"
          width="500" height="339" alt="Pristina
          Library" />
```

3 Edit the tag, and then apply the changes by clicking back in the Design View window

```
Edit tag: <img src="images/pristina2.jpg"
          width="250" height="170" alt="Pristina
          Library" />
```

4 If you enter an incorrect tag, you will be alerted to this by a warning dialog box

Don't forget

In Edit Tag mode, you can edit tags manually, i.e. write the HTML tags yourself, or insert a new tag from the hints menu that appears after a couple of seconds.

Selecting and Removing Tags

Selecting tags

In addition to selecting tags with the Quick Tag Editor, by selecting items in the document window, it is also possible to select them from the tag selector, which is located at the bottom-left of the document window. This enables you to easily identify the opening and closing tags, and also the content that is contained within them. To select tags, using the tag selector:

1 The relevant tags are displayed in the tag selector, which is located at the bottom-left of the document window

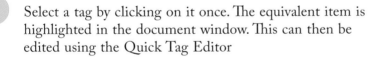

2 Select a tag by clicking on it once. The equivalent item is highlighted in the document window. This can then be edited using the Quick Tag Editor

3 Make changes in the Quick tag editor. These will be applied to the active element on the page

Don't forget

The Quick Tag Editor is a good way to ensure that you select specific tags accurately within the HTML code.

Don't forget

Some tags appear in the tag selector, when items are selected by clicking on them in the document window. Others, such as the "body" tag, are always visible, regardless of what is selected.

Hot tip

The tags displayed in the tag selector can also be used to access the Quick Tag Edit mode. To do this, right-click (Windows) or Ctrl+click (Mac) on the required tag, in the tag selector; the Quick Tag Editor will open in Edit mode, using the selected tag.

...cont'd

Removing tags

Elements on a page can also be removed using the tag selector. To do this:

 Select an element on a page

The tag selector can...

...be used to edit elements on the page

`<body> <h1> <img>`

2 Right-click (Windows) or Ctrl+click (Mac) on one of the tags in the tag selector, and select Remove Tag from the contextual menu

Remove Tag
Quick Tag Editor...
Set Class ▸
Set ID ▸
Code Navigator...
Convert Inline CSS to Rule...
Collapse Full Tag
Collapse Outside Full Tag

3 The item is removed from the page.

The tag selector can...

...be used to edit elements on the page

`<body> <h1>`

4 Working with Images

This chapter gives an overview of using images on the web, and explains how to use and edit them in Dreamweaver, including editing them with Photoshop.

Web Image Overview

When the web was first being developed, it was considered a significant achievement to transfer plain, unformatted text from one computer to another. However, things have moved on considerably from then, and the web is now awash with complex graphics, animations, and sounds, to name but a few of the multimedia effects that are now available to the web designer.

Despite the range of items that can be used on web pages, graphics are still by far the most popular. These can include photographic images, icons, clip art, and even animated graphics. These are all important design elements for web pages, and they should not be overlooked when you are creating a new website.

When graphical formats were being developed for the web, there was a need to create good-quality images that were still small enough to allow them to be downloaded quickly onto the user's computer. This resulted in two file formats that offer good quality, while still creating small file sizes. These are Graphics Interchange Format (GIF) and Joint Photographic Experts Group (JPEG). Some points to bear in mind about both of these formats are:

- JPEGs use up to 16 million colors, and so are best suited for photographic images

- GIFs use 256 colors, and so are best suited for images that do not contain a lot of color definition, such as images with blocks of similar color

- One variety of GIF (GIF 89a) can be used to create images with transparent backgrounds

- Both GIFs and JPEGs use forms of compression to make the file size smaller

Another, more recent, image format for the Web is PNG (Portable Network Graphics). It uses 16 million colors and lossless compression. There are a couple of points to consider with PNGs:

- Not all browsers support the PNG format

- PNG files can contain metatags, indexing information that can be read by web search engines when someone is looking for your website

Hot tip

If you use an image-editing program, such as Fireworks or Photoshop, images can be optimized, so that the best quality can be matched with the smallest file size, which leads to faster downloading speeds.

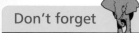

Don't forget

The two types of compression used with image file formats are lossy and lossless. With lossy compression, some image quality is lost, while with lossless compression, it is retained. JPEGs use lossy compression while PNGs use lossless compression.

Using Images Effectively

When you use a program such as Dreamweaver, which gives you the power to quickly and easily insert images into web pages, the temptation is to add them at every opportunity. However, this should be resisted, as it is important to use images carefully and to make the most of their impact and design potential. Some points to bear in mind when using images on web pages are:

- The more images you include, the longer it will take for the user to download your site, i.e. to access it from the host server. This can cause a real problem, because most web users do not have the patience to wait a long time for pages to download. This can be measured in seconds rather than minutes

- Images can be used as the background to a web page, or as independent items within it. Either way, the file size of the image will determine the downloading time

- Keep the on-screen size of images small. Again, this can affect the downloading time and it can detract from other content on a page

- Do not overuse images that spin, blink, or flicker. While this can create a positive initial effect, it can become extremely irritating after it has been viewed several times

- Use images for a specific purpose, i.e. to convey information or as a design feature

- Do not use images that could be deemed offensive or derogatory to any individuals or groups

- Use the same image, or groups of images, to achieve a consistent look throughout a website

- Do not use images just for the sake of it, or just because you can. Users will soon realize that the images are not serving a useful purpose

- Do not use images at the expense of core information. Users may want to find a piece of contact information, rather than look at a lot of images

Beware

Do not make your website too dependent on images, since users can set their browsers so that they do not display any graphics.

Inserting Images

Obtaining images

Images for insertion in a website can be obtained from a variety of sources:

- System clip-art collections. Most computers come with some items of clip art already pre-installed

- CD-ROMs. There are several CD-ROMs on the market that contain tens of thousands of graphical and photographic images

- Digital cameras. These are affordable for the home user, and offer a versatile option for creating your own images for a web page

- Scanners. These can be used to capture existing images in a digital format

Inserting images

Hot tip

To use an image for the background of a page, select Modify, Page Properties, from the menu bar. Click on the Browse button next to the Background Image box, and select an image in the same way as for inserting it directly onto a page. To create a watermark effect, use an image-editing program to make the image semi-transparent, and then insert it as the background.

1 Insert the cursor at the point on the page where you want the image, and click on the Image button on the Common tab of the Insert panel

2 Locate the image you want to use, and click on OK (Windows) or Choose (Mac)

3 Enter the Alternative text for the image. This is an accessibility feature

Image Properties

When an image is selected in Dreamweaver, the Properties Inspector displays information about that image. To access the Image Properties Inspector:

 Select an image by clicking on it once

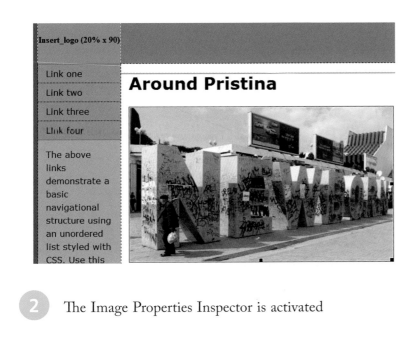

Don't forget

When an image is inserted on a page in Dreamweaver, it only really inserts a reference to where the image is located on your computer, rather than the image itself being physically inserted. This reference is denoted by the <src> tag.

2 The Image Properties Inspector is activated

File details | Image dimensions | Image location | Alternative text

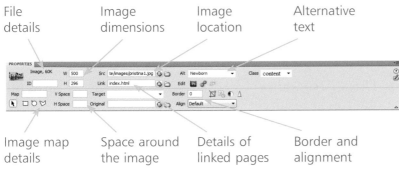

Image map details | Space around the image | Details of linked pages | Border and alignment

Don't forget

Using alternative ("alt") text in place of an image is important, for people who choose not to view images or who are visually impaired and use a reader to view the web. Type a description of the image in the Alt box. This can be a couple of words or several sentences.

Aligning Images and Text

During the process of creating a website, there will be several occasions when you will want to combine images and text. This could be to include a textual definition of an image, or to wrap a block of text around an image, in the style of a newspaper or a magazine article. This can be done through the use of various Dreamweaver functions (see the margin note), or an image can have a value assigned to it, so that it deals with text alignment in a certain way. To align an image and text together:

1 Select an image by clicking on it once. It may already have text around it, or the text can be added later:

Around Pristina

Newborn

2 The alignment options can be selected from the Properties Inspector

The options for aligning images and text are:

- Default. This varies between browsers, but it usually aligns the text baseline with the image base

- Baseline. This aligns the baseline with the image base

- Top. This aligns the tallest point of the text with the top of the image

- Middle. This aligns the text baseline with the middle of the image

Hot tip

One of the most versatile ways of aligning and laying out images and text is through the use of tables. This will enable you to produce precise alignment. The alignment options on this page can also be applied to images and text, once they are inserted into a table. For more on tables, see Chapter 8.

Don't forget

The baseline of a text block is the line on which the bottom of most of the letters sit. This does not include descenders (such as in "g" and "j"), which extend below the baseline.

- Bottom. This aligns the baseline of the text with the bottom of the image

- TextTop. This aligns the tallest point of the text with the top of the image (it usually produces the same effect as Top)

- Absolute Middle. This aligns the middle of the text block with the middle of the image

- Absolute Bottom. This aligns the bottom of the text, including descenders, with the bottom of the image

- Left. This places the image to the left of any text that is next to it. The text will then wrap around the image

- Right. This places the image to the right of any text that is next to it

Alignment buttons

As well as using the alignment options described above, it is also possible to align images and text by using the alignment buttons, in the Image Properties Inspector. Even though this is done by selecting an image, the alignment is applied to the text:

Image with the Top alignment option

Image with the Middle alignment option

Beware

Aligning images and text can create some interesting, and sometimes unwanted, effects. Experiment with different settings until you feel confident about each combination.

Don't forget

Another use for images is the "trace" option. This is where a design has been created, and is then inserted onto a web page as a background for the web designer to copy, or trace over. The trace image does not appear on the published page, and it is really only a guide for the Web designer to follow. To use a trace image, select Modify, Page Properties from the menu bar and, in the Tracing Image window, select the trace image as you would for any other image. There are also options for applying certain levels of transparency.

75

Editing Images

Since images are an integral part of websites, it is important to be able to edit them as quickly and efficiently as possible, when working within the web authoring environment. Dreamweaver achieves this by allowing one-click access to image-editing programs, and also by providing some image-editing functionality within Dreamweaver itself.

Accessing external image editors

Hot tip

The default image editor can be specified in the File Types / Editors window within the Preferences panel.

Don't forget

Sharpening is an image-editing technique that can improve the clarity of images that are slightly blurry. Moderate sharpening can improve most digital images.

76

Beware

Once image-editing commands have been set within Dreamweaver, these are applied to the original image and are permanent. However, the editing can be undone by selecting Edit, Undo, from the menu bar.

1 Select an image within Dreamweaver

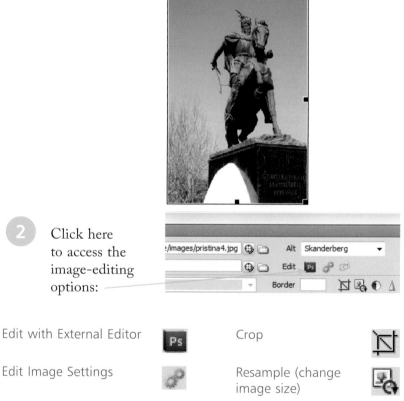

2 Click here to access the image-editing options:

:/images/pristina4.jpg   Alt   Skanderberg

Edit   Ps

Border

Edit with External Editor   Ps

Edit Image Settings

Update from Original

Crop

Resample (change image size)

Brightness and Contrast

Sharpen

Editing with Photoshop

As far as editing images is concerned, previous versions of Dreamweaver were more closely integrated with Fireworks. But in CS5, the main image-editing functions can now be done in Adobe Photoshop, the most popular image-editing program on the market. It is now possible to import Photoshop files (.psd) into Dreamweaver, optimize them for use on the web, and leave the original master file untouched. The original can also be edited, and these changes can be applied to the web version. To do this:

Hot tip

To ensure that you use Photoshop for all of your image-editing functions, select Edit, Preferences, from the menu bar. In the File Types / Editors section, click on the Browse button. Navigate to where Photoshop is located on your hard drive, and select it. This will make it the primary image-editing program when you are working with images in Dreamweaver.

1 Click on the Images, Image button, on the Insert panel

2 Browse to a Photoshop file, i.e. one that has been created with a .psd extension. Select it and click OK (Windows) or Choose (Mac)

3 The Image Preview window enables you to reduce the file size, so that the image can be downloaded more quickly over the Web. Click here to reduce the quality of the image, which will also reduce the file size

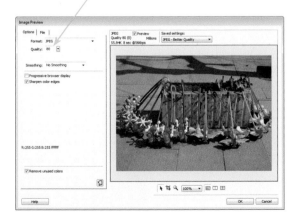

4 Click on the File tab, and enter values in the W and H boxes to reduce the physical size of the image

...cont'd

5 Click OK, and you will have options for saving the image as a web image, e.g. a jpg

Dw Save Web Image

Save as type: Image Files (*.jpg;*.jpeg)

6 The image is placed into the Dreamweaver file, with this icon in the top left corner. This indicates the web version is synchronized with the original

7 The original image can be edited in Photoshop

Don't forget

Selections and layers can also be imported into Dreamweaver from Photoshop. To do this, copy the selection or layer in Photoshop. Return to the Dreamweaver page, and paste the copied item. The Image Preview window will be activated, enabling you to optimize the selection, for use on the web.

8 A red arrow appears on the web version of the image, indicating that the original has been edited, but the web version has not yet been updated

9 Click here on the Properties Inspector to update the web version of the image

10 The version of the image in Dreamweaver is updated to match the original

Creating Rollover Images

One of the most eye-catching effects with images on the Web, is the creation of rollovers. This is where two images are combined, although only one is visible initially on the page. However, when the cursor is moved over the image, it is replaced by the second one. To make this even more impressive, a hyperlink can be added to the rollover, so that the user can click on it and be taken to another page within the site, or a different site altogether.

Until recently, rollovers were the preserve of designers who could use programming languages, such as Javascript. However, Dreamweaver overcomes this by allowing you to create rollovers, while generating all of the script in the background. This means that you have a powerful design tool at your disposal, without having to delve into computer-language scripting.

Creating a rollover image

1. Create the two images that you want to use for the rollover. Make sure they are the same dimensions, because they will be produced at the same size in the rollover

2. Insert the cursor where you want the rollover to appear

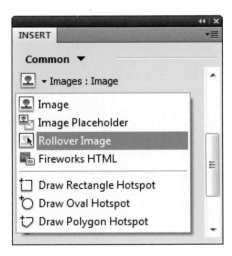

3. Select the Rollover Image button on the Insert panel

Beware

Do not get too carried away with using rollovers, although this can be difficult to resist when you first learn how to create them. As with any item on a web page that moves or changes from one thing to another, a little goes a long way.

Hot tip

If you are using a rollover to link to another page, or site on the web, choose your images carefully, so that users can quickly relate the image with the link that it contains. Otherwise, they may think that it is just a clever graphical effect.

...cont'd

Hot tip

One effective device is to use the same image for both the initial image and the rollover one. However, edit the rollover image to be a different color, or to have some degree of transparency. This will then produce a subtle effect when the rollover is activated.

Don't forget

URL stands for Uniform Resource Locator, and it is a unique address for every page on the Web. It is usually in a format similar to http://www.mysite.com. If you are linking to a page on your own site, you only need to insert the page name, e.g. news.htm. But if you want to link to an external website, you will need to insert the full web address (URL).

Don't forget

To test a rollover, save the file, and press F12, or select File, Preview in Browser from the menu bar, and select a browser.

 Click here to enter a name for the rollover button

5 Click here to locate the first image you are going to use. Repeat the process by clicking the button below, for the second image

6 If you want users to be able to go to another web page when they click, enter a file in the "When clicked, Go to URL" box. Click OK to create the rollover

7 When viewed in a browser, the image will look like this, initially...

...and this when the cursor moves over it

5 Using CSS

Cascading style sheets (CSS) are sets of rules that can be used to format the content of HTML documents. This chapter introduces the elements of CSS, shows how to create pages with CSS, and details how to attach CSS to HTML documents in Dreamweaver. It also shows how you can preview how pages will look, using the Adobe BrowserLab.

CSS Overview

In the early days of web design, the majority of pages were created with HTML code. This specified the content and formatting within the same document. However, this could be cumbersome, in that each time there was a change in formatting, this would have to be included in the HTML document. For instance, each time a different font was used, this had to be specified in terms of font family, size, and color.

In recent years, cascading style sheets (CSS) have become a lot more popular for designing web pages. This is because they can be used to separate the content and presentation of web pages. The content is still in the HTML document, but the presentation (or formatting) is included within the CSS document in the form of a group of formatting rules. These can then be applied to multiple files. This means that if one of the rules is updated, the appearance of the relevant content in all of the linked files is also updated, without the need to edit the individual HTML files. CSS rules can be used for formatting and positioning items.

A CSS rule consists of two parts: the selector and the declaration. The selector refers to the rule that is being created or defined, and the declaration refers to the elements of the rule. CSS styles can be imported directly into an HTML document, in which case, they are usually located in the <head> section of the document, or they can be created in specific CSS files. These have a .css extension, and can be linked to the HTML document.

CSS elements

Hot tip

For a detailed look at working with cascading style sheets, and creating web pages with them, look at "CSS in Easy Steps" in this series.

82

① Selector

```
body{
    font-family: Arial,sans-serif;
    color: #333333;
    line-height: 1.166;
    margin: 0px;
    padding: 0px;
    background: #cccccc url(bg_grad.jpg) fixed;
}
```

② Declaration (within the {} brackets)

CSS in Dreamweaver

Dreamweaver CS5 has been developed to maximize the use of style sheets in the creation of web pages, and to make them as easy to use and manipulate as possible. This is done using the Properties Inspector and the CSS Styles panel:

1. Click here, on the Properties Inspector, to edit specific CSS rules

2. Click here to access the CSS Styles panel

3. Use the CSS Styles panel to create, add, and edit style sheets. The properties of included style sheets are displayed within this panel

Don't forget

In Dreamweaver CS5, there is more emphasis on using CSS rather than just plain HTML code. However, traditional HTML coding is still catered for, either on its own, for content and presentation, or in conjunction with style sheets, for formatting.

83

4. Within Design View, complex CSS designs are displayed, even if the CSS rules are contained in a separate .css file

CSS and HTML

Although CSS and HTML are separate, but related, items of a web page, Dreamweaver CS5 has features that enable you to work with both of them, as efficiently as possible. HTML and CSS buttons are now located on the Properties Inspector, so that it is possible to quickly toggle between the two. Generally, HTML allows you to insert certain tags, while the CSS button provides the means to format the content on a page. To use HTML and CSS:

Don't forget

When using CSS, the content for a web page is still contained within the HTML file. The style sheet specifies the appearance of the content, and can be in the source file or a linked (related) one.

1 Enter content, and click on the HTML button on the Properties Inspector

Heading 1

PROPERTIES
<> HTML Format Heading 1 ▾
CSS   ID   None ▾

2 Click on the CSS button to apply and access CSS elements

CSS

3 Click on the CSS Panel button to activate this panel

PROPERTIES
<> HTML   Targeted Rule <New CSS Rule> ▾
CSS   Edit Rule   CSS Panel

4 Click on the Edit Rule button to edit a specific CSS rule, or to create a new one

5 CSS Rules can be created and edited in the New CSS Rule window

New CSS Rule:
Selector Type:
Choose a contextual selector type for your CSS rule.
Tag (redefines an HTML element) ▾   OK
                                                 Cancel
Selector Name:
Choose or enter a name for your selector.
h1 ▾
This selector name will apply your rule to
all <h1> elements.

Less Specific   More Specific

Rule Definition:
Choose where your rule will be defined.
(This document only) ▾   Help

6 CSS Rules are displayed in the CSS Styles panel

CSS STYLES

| All | Current |

Summary for Selection

font-family	Tahoma, Geneva, sans-...
font-size	36px
color	#000

Rules

| h1 | <h1> |

Properties for "h1"

color	#000
font-family	Tahoma, Geneva, sans-s...
font-size	36px
Add Property	

Don't forget

CSS styles can be created for formatting specific elements within a page (such as applying formatting to a piece of text). These are known as class styles. The formatting for entire tags, such as the <p> tag, can also be specified with style sheets.

7 Changes are made within the Properties section of the CSS Styles panel

Properties for "h1"

color	#906
font-family	Tahoma, Geneva, sans-s...
font-size	36px
Add Property	

85

8 The CSS code is added to the HTML file

```
h1 {
    font-family: Tahoma, Geneva, sans-serif;
    font-size: 36px;
    color: #000;
}
</style></head>

<body>
<h1>Heading 1</h1>
```

9 The formatting is added to the content

Heading 1

Elements of CSS

When working with CSS, there are certain elements within Dreamweaver that are important for creating and editing style sheets. To access these:

Don't forget

Click on the link button on the CSS panel to link to an external style sheet, i.e. one that has already been created. Click on the icon to the right (with the plus sign on it), to create a new rule, either for an external style sheet or within the current file.

1 Open the CSS Styles panel by selecting Window, CSS Styles, from the menu bar, or by clicking on the CSS button on the Properties Inspector

Style sheet rules are displayed here

Rule properties are displayed here

CSS STYLES

| All | Current |

All Rules

- `<style>`
  - body
  - ul, ol, dl
  - h1, h2, h3, h4, h5, h6, p
  - a img
  - a:link
  - a:visited
  - a:hover, a:active, a:focus
  - .container

Properties for "h1, h2, h3, h4, h5, h6, p"

color	■ #000
font-family	Verdana, Geneva, sans-serif
margin-top	0
padding-left	15px
padding-right	15px
Add Property	

2 Click on the link button (left-hand button) to attach existing style sheets, or click on the add button (right-hand button) to start creating new style sheets

3 In the New CSS Rule dialog box, click here to create a class rule. This is a uniquely named style that can be applied to specific items in an HTML document

New CSS Rule

Selector Type:
Choose a contextual selector type for your CSS rule.

Class (can apply to any HTML element)

| OK |
| Cancel |

Selector Name:
Choose or enter a name for your selector.

Less Specific | More Specific

Rule Definition:
Choose where your rule will be defined.

(This document only)

| Help |

4 Click here to create a rule for an existing HTML tag. This creates properties for the tag that are applied within the whole document. For instance, rules can be created for the <body> tag, the <p> tag, or the heading tags

Selector Type:

Choose a contextual selector type for your CSS rule.

Tag (redefines an HTML element) ▼

Selector Name:

Choose or enter a name for your selector.

h2

5 Click OK, in the New CSS Rule dialog box, to access the CSS Rule Definition dialog box. Enter the properties for the CSS rule, and click OK to create the rule. This will be available in the CSS Styles panel

CSS Rule definition for .red_text   ✕

Category	Type
Type	
Background	Font-family: Tahoma, Geneva, sans-serif ▼
Block	
Box	Font-size: medium ▼ px ▼ Font-weight: ▼
Border	
List	Font-style: ▼ Font-variant: ▼
Positioning	
Extensions	Line-height: ▼ px ▼ Text-transform: ▼

Text-decoration: ☐ underline   Color: ■ #F00
               ☐ overline
               ☐ line-through
               ☐ blink
               ☑ none

Help   OK   Cancel   Apply

Don't forget

If you create new rules for an existing HTML tag, these rules will apply to all of the affected content in the HTML document. For instance, if the font for the <p> tag is specified as Verdana, any text that appears within this tag will be in Verdana.

Don't forget

The CSS Rule Definition dialog box only contains some of the elements that can be used in style sheets. For a full list of styles, access the O'Reilly CSS Reference panel (Window, Results, Reference from the menu bar) and view the styles in the Styles drop-down box.

CSS Layouts

When creating pages with a CSS layout, there are a number of predesigned layouts that can be used as the foundation for the pages. These are HTML pages that have had the relevant CSS rules applied to them, so that they display certain formatting. These layouts contain columns that are created in different ways. These are:

- Fixed. This creates columns at a specific size, in pixels

- Elastic. This creates columns that change size, if the text size is increased in the browser in which they are being viewed. They do not change size if the browser window is resized

- Liquid. This creates columns that change size if the browser window, in which they are being viewed, is changed in size

- Hybrid. This creates columns in a combination of the first three options

To create a page with a CSS layout:

Hot tip

Test CSS layouts in different browsers, to see how the various layout options appear.

88

1 Select File, New, from the menu bar

2 Select the Blank Page option and HTML as the Page Type

New Document

Page Type:

Blank Page

HTML
HTML template

3 Select a CSS layout

Layout:

<none>
1 column fixed, centered
1 column fixed, centered, header and foot
1 column liquid, centered
1 column liquid, centered, header and foot
2 column fixed, left sidebar
2 column fixed, left sidebar, header and fo
2 column fixed, right sidebar
2 column fixed, right sidebar, header and f
2 column liquid, left sidebar
2 column liquid, left sidebar, header and fo

4 Click on Create

5 The page is created with the CSS layout and draft content, to show the formatting of the page

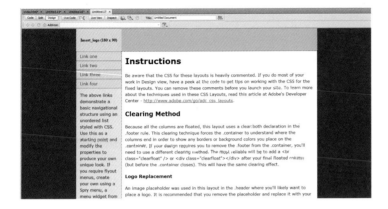

6 By default, the CSS formatting is inserted in the head part of the HTML file

```
<head>
<meta http-equiv="Content-Type" content="text/html; charset=utf-8" />
<title>Untitled Document</title>
<style type="text/css">
<!--
body {
    font: 100%/1.4 Verdana, Arial, Helvetica, sans-serif;
    background: #42413C;
    margin: 0;
    padding: 0;
    color: #000;
}

/* ~~ Element/tag selectors ~~ */
ul, ol, dl { /* Due to variations between browsers, it's best practices
 items (LI, DT, DD) they contain. Remember that what you do here will c
    padding: 0;
    margin: 0;
}
h1, h2, h3, h4, h5, h6, p {
    margin-top: 0;   /* removing the top margin gets around an issue wh
follow. */
    padding-right: 15px;
    padding-left: 15px; /* adding the padding to the sides of the eleme
 also be used as an alternate method. */
}
a img { /* this selector removes the default blue border displayed in s
    border: none;
}

/* ~~ Styling for your site's links must remain in this order - includi
a:link {
```

Hot tip

Instead of having the CSS formatting inserted in the head of the HTML file, it is also possible to create a new CSS file for it, or link to an existing CSS file, to use additional formatting. This can be done in the New Document window (steps 2 and 3 on the previous page).

CSS Inspector

The CSS Inspector is a function that works with the Live View option, to enable you to view and edit elements of CSS code within your files. This can be done within the same environment, so you can clearly identify CSS elements and see where they are in the code, and also in the CSS Styles panel. To use CSS Inspect:

1 With Live View activated, click on the Inspect button

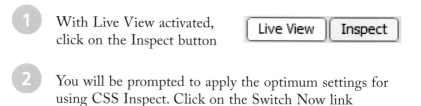

2 You will be prompted to apply the optimum settings for using CSS Inspect. Click on the Switch Now link

ⓘ Inspect mode is most useful with certain workspace settings. Switch now | More Info...

3 The following settings are applied for CSS Inspect

4 In CSS Inspect, the code is highlighted yellow. Make sure the CSS Styles panel is visible

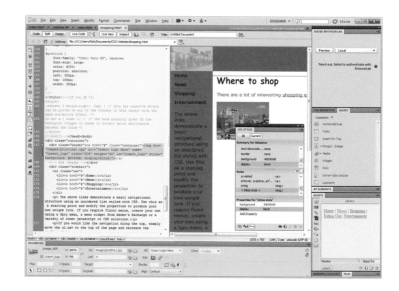

Don't forget

The optimum settings for Inspect mode are with the CSS Styles panel open, Split View enabled, Live View enabled, and Live Code enabled.

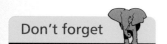

5 CSS Inspect mode is read-only, and you cannot edit in this mode. The Properties Inspector is therefore grayed-out. If you make any changes, CSS Inspect will exit

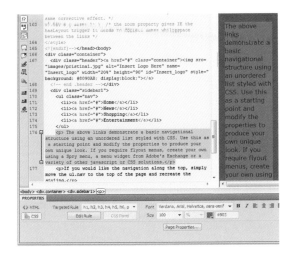

6 In CSS Inspect mode, rollover an element in Design View. The related code is highlighted in Code View

Don't forget

To edit an item in CSS Inspect mode, click on the item you want to edit. Inspect mode will then exit, so that you can make the changes.

91

7 As you rollover an element, the related CSS rules and properties are displayed in the CSS Styles panel. If you rollover another element, the CSS Styles panel will update accordingly

...cont'd

8. To edit an element of CSS, first identify it in CSS Inspect mode

Don't forget

When you click on an item in Inspect mode, the Inspect button becomes inactive. Code view remains yellow, as Live Code is still active.

9. Rollover it in CSS Inspect mode. Click on the element to enable editing for this element. This will cause CSS Inspect mode to exit, but Live View will still be active

10. The CSS Styles panel displays the properties of the currently selected style

Properties for "h1, h2, h3, h4, h5, h6, p"	
color	#906
margin-top	0
padding-left	15px
padding-right	15px
Add Property	

11. Make editing changes in the CSS Styles panel

Properties for "h1, h2, h3, h4, h5, h6, p"	
color	#009
margin-top	0
padding-left	15px
padding-right	15px
Add Property	

12. The changes are applied to the page

CSS Disable/Enable

Since CSS rules can have numerous properties, there can be times when you want to remove specific elements, while retaining the rest of the properties of a rule. This can be done by disabling elements within the CSS Styles panel. To do this:

 1 Select an element on the page

The above links demonstrate a basic navigational structure using an unordered

2 The rule and its properties are displayed in the CSS Styles panel

3 Check next to a rule to disable it. A red circle with a line through it indicates the rule has been disabled

4 In Design View, the element is displayed with the disabled rules turned off. Click on the red circle icon in the CSS Styles panel to enable the rule

The above links demonstrate a basic navigational structure using an unordered list styled with CSS.

Beware

If a rule is disabled in the CSS Styles panel, it is removed from the related code within the file, or the related file, if this is where it is located.

Code Navigator

Simplifying CSS is a feature of the development of Dreamweaver, and, in CS5, the Code Navigator is another major step forward in making CSS clearer and more accessible. To access and use the Code Navigator:

Hot tip

The Code Navigator can also be accessed by Alt+clicking (Windows) or Command+Option +click (Mac) within the selected element.

1 Insert the cursor in an element on the page

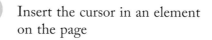

2 After a couple of seconds, the Code Navigator wheel appears. Click on it

3 All of the CSS rules applied to the piece of content are displayed.

```
index.html
    body
    .container
    .sidebar1
    ul, ol, dl
    ul
    ul.nav
    ul.nav li
    a:visited
    a:hover, a:active, a:focus
    ul.nav a, ul.nav a:visited
    ul.nav a:hover, ul.nav a:active, ul.nav a:focus
css_management.css
    a:link

Alt+click to show                    Disable   indicator
```

4 Rollover a rule to display its properties

```
index.html
    body
    .cont        font: 100%/1.4 Verdana, Arial, Helvetica, sans-serif;
    .sideb       background: #4E5869;
    ul, ol,      margin: 0;
    ul           padding: 0;
    ul.nav       color: #000;
    ul nav
```

5 Click on an item to view it in Code View

```
8    body {
9        font: 100%/1.4 Verdana, Arial, Helvetica,
    sans-serif;
10       background: #4E5869;
11       margin: 0;
12       padding: 0;
13       color: #000;
```

6 Properties can also be edited in the CSS Styles panel

Properties for "body"	
background	#4E5869
color	■ #000
font	100%/1.4 Verdana, Arial, He...
margin	0
padding	0
Add Property	

Beware

CSS rules and properties cannot be edited directly in the Code Navigator window. This has to be done by clicking on an item, as shown in Step 7.

95

7 If other style sheets are also attached to the item selected in Step 2, this will also be displayed in the Code Navigator

css_management.css
a:link

8 Click on this link to open and view the related CSS file

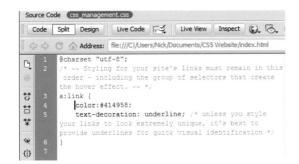

9 In the Code Navigator, check on the Disable box, to disable the Code Navigator wheel from appearing automatically

✓ Disable ✸ indicator

Including Style Sheets

There are two ways in which style sheet formatting can be included within an HTML document. One is to include the style sheet elements within the HTML document itself, and the other is to create an external style sheet, and link this to the HTML document. This can be specified when an element for a style sheet is being created:

Don't forget

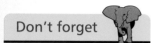

The <head> section of an HTML document is the one that contains information about the document not usually displayed when viewed in a browser. It comes before the <body> section and can contain information, such as metadata (for search engines), document type and title, and any embedded CSS code.

1 Select File, New, from the menu bar, and make the appropriate selection in the New Document window

2 In the Layout CSS list, select whether you want to add the CSS to the current document (Add to Head) or Create a New File (this example is for a new file)

Layout CSS: Create New File

Attach CSS file:
- Add to Head
- Create New File
- Link to Existing File

3 Click on the Create button   Create

4 Select a folder into which to save the CSS file that will be created. (It is good practise to create a CSS folder within your site structure)

Hot tip

In general, it is better practice to link to style sheets in a separate file, rather than including the CSS code within an HTML file. This is because it reduces the size of the HTML file, and also because it makes it easier to update a lot of linked files, as the changes only have to be made in the single CSS file, rather than in every individual HTML file.

Save Style Sheet File As

Save in: css

Name	Date modified	Type
colors5	31/05/2010 9:30 PM	Cascading Style S...
css_management	01/06/2010 2:55 PM	Cascading Style S...
css1	31/05/2010 8:46 PM	Cascading Style S...
css2	31/05/2010 10:31 ...	Cascading Style S...
css3	01/06/2010 10:15 ...	Cascading Style S...

Recent Places
Desktop
Libraries
Computer
Network

File name: twoColFixLtHdr   Save
Save as type: Style Sheet Files (*.css)   Cancel
Site Root

5 The page is created with the formatting taken from the related CSS file

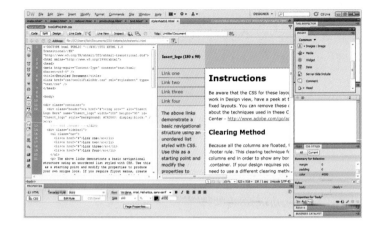

6 The reference to the CSS file is contained within the code of the HTML file

```
6   <link href="css/twoColFixLtHdr.css" rel="stylesheet" type=
    "text/css" />
```

7 Click on the related link for the CSS file, to view the code for the CSS file

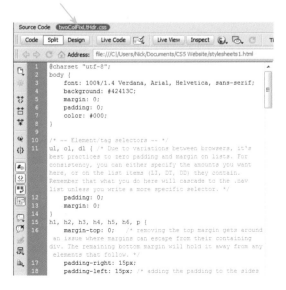

Don't forget

If the CSS is contained within a related file, i.e. a separate CSS file, the source document can be updated by selecting the CSS file on the related links bar, and editing the code as required. Save the CSS file to update the content in the source file, and click on the Refresh button in the source document.

CSS Styles Panel

The CSS Styles panel is a vital item when creating and editing style sheets. All of the rules and properties of associated style sheets are displayed within the CSS Styles panel, and elements can be added and edited here too. If the CSS Styles, panel is not visible, select Window, CSS Styles, from the menu bar, or click the CSS button on the Properties Inspector to open the CSS Styles panel. To use the CSS Styles panel:

Hot tip

Several different style sheets can be attached to a single HTML document. However, if this is done, make sure that each one contains different rules, and that there is no duplication.

1. Click here to display all of the available style sheets for a document and their properties

2. Click here to display the rules of a selected style sheet

3. Click here to select a specific rule within the style sheet

4. Click here to edit one of the properties of the selected rule

5. The changes are made in the CSS Styles panel, and they will also take effect within the style sheet, and any linked documents

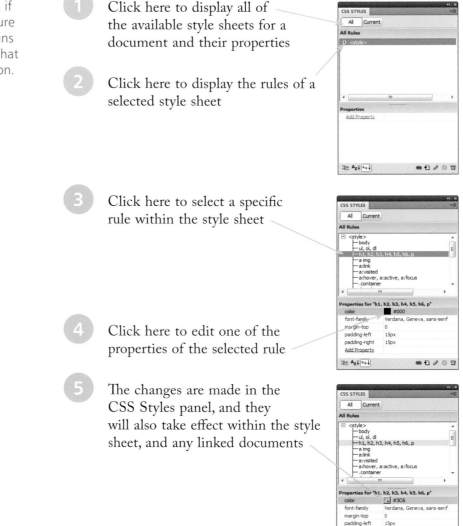

6 Click here to view the style
   sheet details of the currently
   selected item within the
   document

7 The properties of the
   currently selected item are
   displayed here

Don't forget

For more information on
creating and adding CSS
rules and properties, see
Chapter 6.

8 Click here to display the
   properties of a selected item,
   and all of the other available
   CSS properties

Don't forget

The property families
contain all the CSS
properties that can be
used within style sheets.

9 Click here to display the
   property families. Click on a
   plus sign to see the available
   properties for each family

CSS Management

If you work with CSS frequently, there will be times when you want to use a certain piece of CSS in more than one document. It would be feasible to copy and paste the relevant CSS text, but Dreamweaver provides the means to manage all of your CSS code, through the CSS panel. To do this:

1 Click a rule in the CSS panel

2 Click here, and select Move CSS Rules from the menu

Go to Code

New...

Edit...

Duplicate...

Rename Class...

Edit Selector

Move CSS Rules...

3 Click on the "Style sheet" button and then the Browse button, to select an existing style sheet

4 Click on the "A new style sheet" button and click OK

5 Create a new style sheet within your website structure. The new rule will be included in the new file

Browser Compatibility Check

As there are now an increasing number of browsers on the
market, it is important to check how CSS content will perform
on each of the different platforms (because of its complexity, CSS
code can be rendered differently on different browsers). Within
Dreamweaver, there is a facility to check the compatibility of CSS
in different browsers. To do this:

1   From the menu bar, select File, Check Page,
    Browser Compatibility

2   Any
    compatibility
    issues are
    displayed
    here

3   If there are no compatibility
    issues, this is noted in the
    bottom-left of the window

    No issues detected.

4   Click on this button to change the settings for
    the browsers to be checked

5   Specify the versions of different browsers to be
    checked, and click OK

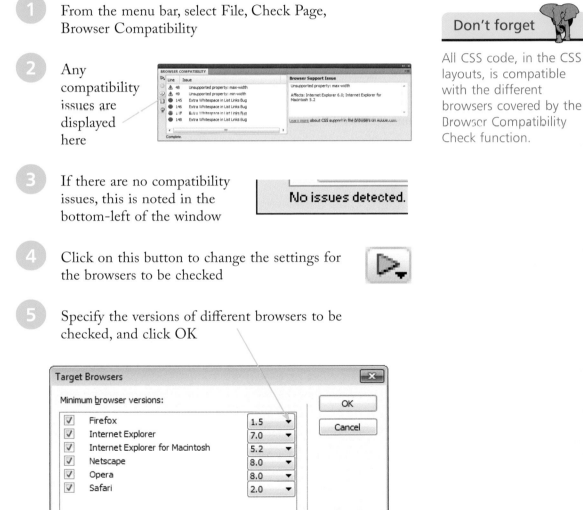

Don't forget

All CSS code, in the CSS
layouts, is compatible
with the different
browsers covered by the
Browser Compatibility
Check function.

101

CSS Advisor

CSS can be a complicated, and constantly developing subject, if you want to start writing and using your own rules. However, help is at hand, in the form of an online CSS forum called the CSS Advisor. This has discussions about the latest CSS issues and uses, and it is somewhere to swap ideas and experiences with like-minded CSS users. To access the CSS Advisor:

Don't forget

Even if you do not post any questions on the CSS Advisor site, it is worth looking at it, just to see what other designers are talking about.

1 Access the Browser Compatibility Check window, as shown on the previous page

2 Click on the Check Adobe.com link to access the CSS Advisor site

3 Click on one of the subjects, to view all of the relevant posts and comments. It is also possible to submit your own posts about a CSS topic

Adobe BrowserLab

With the ever increasing number of web browsers available, and the wider functionality of web pages, it is important to be able to preview designs as they would appear in a variety of browsers. This can be done by using the online Adobe BrowserLab. To use this:

1 Open a file and click here, on the menu bar, and click on the Preview in Adobe BrowserLab link

2 The BrowserLab is accessed

3 The page is displayed as it will be rendered in the currently selected browser

4 The currently selected browser is displayed underneath the View button

Don't forget

Abobe BrowserLab is part of the CS Live online service. To access this, you need to obtain an Adobe ID and to register for CS Live. This can be done at www.adobe.com

103

...cont'd

5 Click on the current browser, and select other browser options. Click on the All Browsers link to see the full list of available browsers

Don't forget

The browsers that are included within the BrowserLab are Chrome, Firefox, Internet Explorer, and Safari. For Internet Explorer, it goes back to version 6.

6 Click on the View button, to select other options for how you would like the page to be displayed

7 Click on the 2-up View in Step 6, and select another browser, to see how the page will look in different browsers

8 Select Onion Skin in Step 6, to see how closely the formatting matches in different browsers

9 Drag this slider to determine the amount of transparency between the two pages

6 Formatting with CSS

This chapter shows how to format content in HTML files, through the use of CSS. It covers creating and editing style sheets, and also details the different types of CSS rules that can be created and applied. The concept of positioning items with CSS is also covered.

Formatting Text with CSS

For many years, text on web pages was formatted by applying tags to the HTML code, such as 'font' tags. However, formatting with CSS is now considerd to be a more robust way of displaying text: it can be applied consistently across a site, and is now a recognized standard across the web. One way to format text using CSS is to first apply a format in HTML, such as Paragraph or Heading 1, and then style this format using CSS. To do this:

Don't forget

Elements, such as font, size, weight, color, and alignment, are specified within CSS rules, rather than the HTML code.

1 In the Properties Inspector, click on the HTML button

2 Enter the text

3 At this point, there is no format applied

```
8    <body>
9    Text can be added and formatted using CSS.
10   </body>
11   </html>
```

4 Click on the HTML Format box and select a format (in this example, Paragraph, which is denoted in the code by the <p> tag)

5 In the Properties Inspector, click on the CSS button. At this point, there is no formatting applied. Click on the down arrow in the Font box

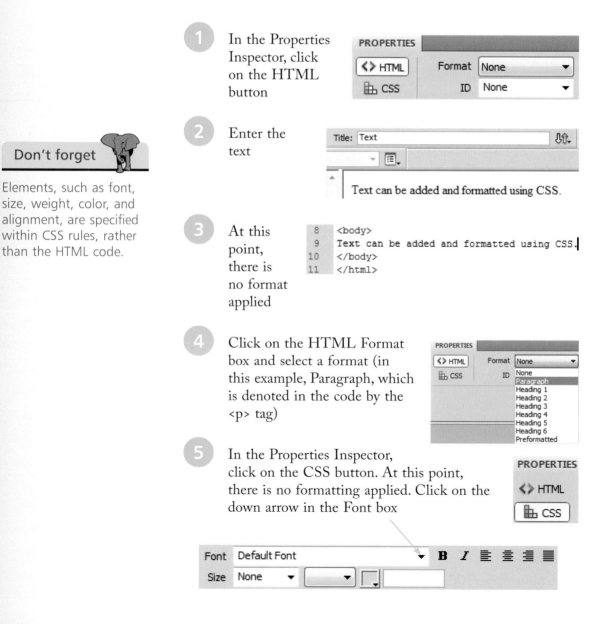

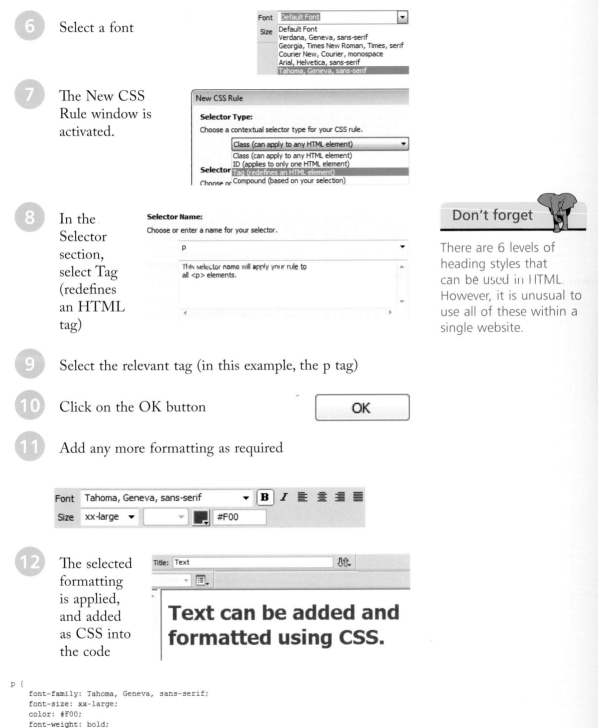

6 Select a font

7 The New CSS Rule window is activated.

8 In the Selector section, select Tag (redefines an HTML tag)

Don't forget

There are 6 levels of heading styles that can be used in HTML. However, it is unusual to use all of these within a single website.

9 Select the relevant tag (in this example, the p tag)

10 Click on the OK button

11 Add any more formatting as required

12 The selected formatting is applied, and added as CSS into the code

Text can be added and formatted using CSS.

```
p {
    font-family: Tahoma, Geneva, sans-serif;
    font-size: xx-large;
    color: #F00;
    font-weight: bold;
}
```

Attaching a Style Sheet

One of the quickest ways of adding CSS to a web page is to attach a style sheet to an existing HTML document. This can be done with a style sheet that you have created yourself, or there are sample ones contained within Dreamweaver that can be used. To do this:

1 Open the CSS Styles panel, and click here to attach an external style sheet

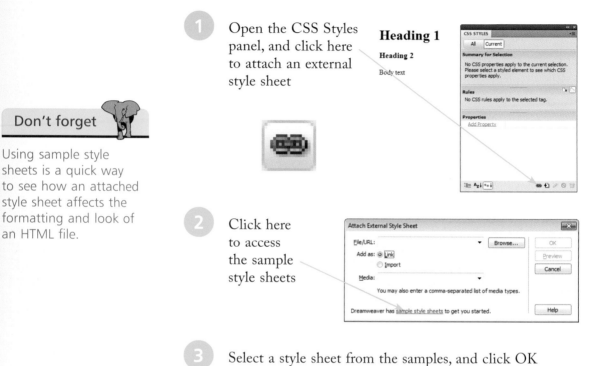

Don't forget

Using sample style sheets is a quick way to see how an attached style sheet affects the formatting and look of an HTML file.

2 Click here to access the sample style sheets

3 Select a style sheet from the samples, and click OK

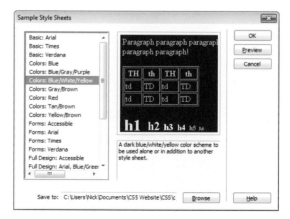

4 Details of the attached style sheet are displayed in the CSS Styles panel. Click here to show and hide all of the rules within the style sheet

109

Hot tip

When a sample style sheet is attached, it is automatically saved into a new folder within the current site structure. By default, the folder name is CSS.

5 When content is added to the page, it takes on the appropriate style from the style sheet. For instance, when body content is added, it takes on the properties of the "body" rule in the style sheet. Similarly, if styles, such as "h1", are applied, these take on the properties of the corresponding rule in the style sheet

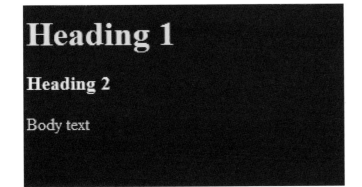

Heading 1

Heading 2

Body text

Creating a Style Sheet

In addition to using sample style sheets, it is also possible to create your own style sheets for a document. This can be done by manually writing the CSS code, but an easier way is to create it by using the CSS Styles panel. To do this:

Hot tip

To open predesigned page designs based on style sheets, select File, New, from the menu bar, and select Page from Sample, CSS Style Sheet.

Beware

If you use an external style sheet to format a web page or a website, make sure that you upload the style sheet file(s), as well as the HTML files, when you are publishing the site.

1 Open the CSS Styles panel, and click here

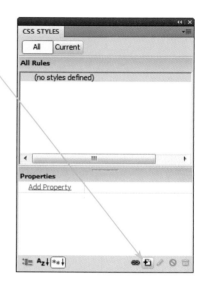

2 Select an option for creating a new rule within a style sheet

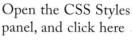

3 Click here to create a new external style sheet, and click OK

④ Select a name and location for the new style sheet, and click Save

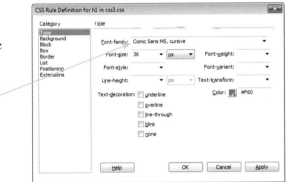

Don't forget

Save a new style sheet in the same site folder as the file to which it is linked, or create a new CSS folder, and save your style sheets there.

⑤ Enter the properties for the rule selected in step 2, and click OK

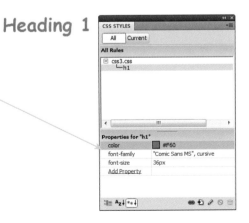

Hot tip

Click the Apply button to see style changes as they are made, without leaving the CSS Rule Definition window.

⑥ Details of the newly created style sheet are displayed in the CSS Styles panel. The properties, for the rule created in step 5, are displayed here

Heading 1

Editing Style Sheets

The CSS Styles panel provides great flexibility for editing style sheets, once they have been created and attached to a document:

Beware

Coding for CSS files is a lot stricter than for HTML files: if one element of the code syntax is missing, or entered in the wrong place, then that part of the code will not function.

1. Open the CSS Styles panel, and select a style sheet or a rule within it

2. Click here to edit the style sheet file

3. The style sheet is opened as a separate document (denoted by a .css extension). Elements of the style sheet can then be directly edited within the code of the style sheet

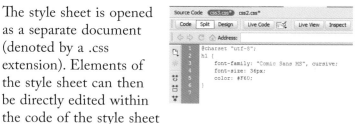

Editing with the CSS Styles panel

Elements can also be edited using the CSS Styles panel:

Don't forget

Changes made directly within a CSS file have to be saved before they take effect.

1. Select a rule within an attached style sheet. The rule's properties are displayed here

2 Select a property within the style, and click here to edit the rules of the property

Properties for "h1"

color	#F60
font-family	
font-size	
Add Property	

#0C3

3 The new attributes for the property are displayed within the CSS Styles panel. This will also have been updated in the style sheet file, and in the design

Heading 1

CSS STYLES

All | Current

All Rules

css3.css
└─ h1

Properties for "h1"

color	#0C3
font-family	"Comic Sans MS", cursive
font-size	36px
Add Property	

Hot tip

If a CSS rule or property is edited in the CSS Styles panel, the relevant CSS file will be opened and updated automatically, at the same time.

113

4 Click the Add Property link to add a new property to the rule, and enter the attributes for the property

Properties for "h1"

color	#0C3
font-family	"Comic Sans MS", cursive
font-size	36px

background
background-attachm
background-color
background-image
background-position

Adding New CSS Rules

In addition to using the CSS Styles panel to edit the existing rules of a style sheet, you can also use it to add new rules to an existing style sheet. To do this:

Don't forget

Some CSS rules, such as class rules, have to be physically added to content within the HTML files. Other rules, such as those for modifying an existing HTML tag, are automatically applied when the tag is included in a document.

1. Open the CSS Styles panel and select an existing style sheet, or a rule within it

2. Click here to add a new rule

3. Select the type of rule to be created. Make sure the rule is to be defined in an existing style sheet. Click OK

4. Enter the properties for the rule, and click OK

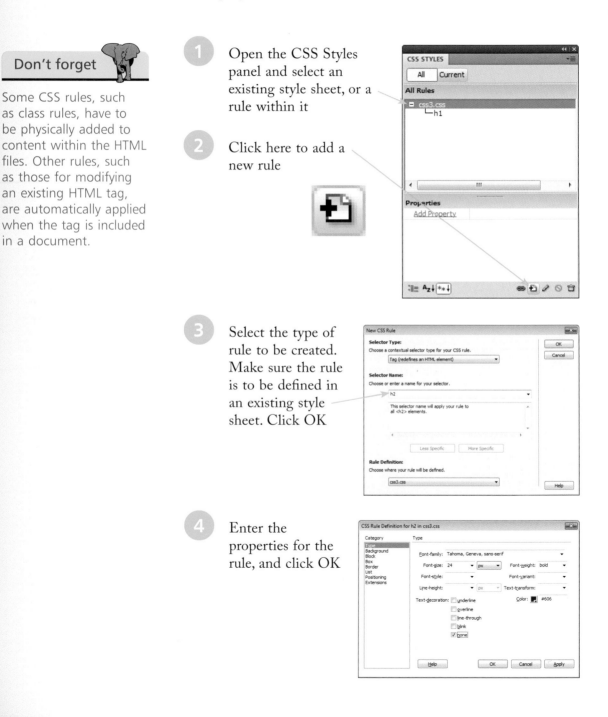

5 The new rule is added here, within the CSS Styles panel

6 The properties for the new rule are displayed here, within the panel

Beware

When a new rule is added to a style sheet via the CSS Styles panel, the style-sheet file is opened and updated automatically. This then has to be saved, to retain the new rule.

7 The new rule and its properties are also added to the CSS file

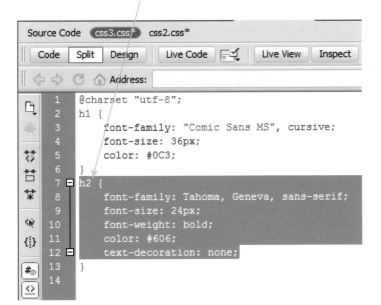

Creating Class Styles

Class styles within a style sheet are rules that are created with unique names, which can then be applied to certain elements of a web page. This can be particularly useful for adding specific formatting to individual elements within a page. For instance, you may want to use red text for emphasis, and this can be achieved by creating an appropriate class style. To create class styles:

Hot tip

A class rule has to be preceded by a period, when it is being named in the New CSS Rule dialog box, and have no spaces in it. The name ".boldblue" is an example of this.

1 Open the CSS Styles panel, and click here to create a new rule

2 Click here to create a new class rule

3 Enter a unique name for the rule, and click OK

4 Enter the properties for the class rule

5 Click OK

6 The class rule and its properties are added to the CSS Styles panel

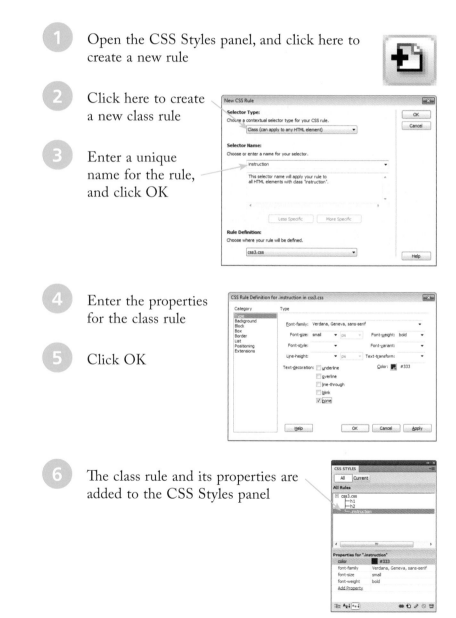

Applying Styles

Once class styles have been created, they can then be applied to elements within the web page. This can be done with any element, including text, images, and tables. To apply class styles:

1 Select a piece of content on a page. For text, this can either be done by clicking within a text block (which applies the style to the whole block) or by highlighting specific text (which applies the style to the highlighted section)

2 Click here, in the Properties Inspector, and select a class style

3 The style is applied to the selected item on the page

Including Div Tags

One way CSS styles can be used to format and position elements on a web page is through the use of div tags. These act as containers for content, and they are particularly useful for positioning items on a page, independently from other elements. To create div tags:

1 Insert the cursor on a page

2 Select Insert Div Tag, from the Insert panel

3 Click on the New CSS Rule button

4 Give the div tag class a name (content), and then enter the properties for the div tag

5 Enter the properties for the div tag, in the CSS Rule Definition window. One useful option for div tags is Positioning. Click OK

6 In the Insert Div Tag window, click OK

7 The div tag is added to the page, at the position specified in CSS Rule Definition window

Heading 1

Content for class "content" id "content" Goes Here

This text contains instructions about
how to fill in the forms.

8 The div tag can be repositioned on the page by clicking and dragging here

Heading 1

This text contains instructions about
how to fill in the forms.

Div tags can be moved by dragging.

Don't forget

Div tags can be edited from within the CSS Styles panel, in the same way as any other CSS element in the panel.

Positioning with CSS

One of the great advantages of CSS is the ability to position items with great accuracy. This can be done with most CSS elements, but the best way to do it is to create a div tag for a particular item, and then apply the positioning to the div tag itself. Any items within the div tag will then be positioned accordingly. To position items with div tags:

Hot tip

A box size does not have to be specified for a div tag. If it is not, the div tag will extend across the whole of the page being created.

120

 Create a div tag, and click on the New CSS Rule button

Don't forget

If "relative" is selected as the type of positioning, the element will be positioned in relation to the previous item in the document's text flow.

2 In the New CSS Rule window, select an ID selector. Click OK

3 Click the Positioning category in the CSS Rule Definition window

4 Set the position for how the box will be placed

Positioning

Position: absolute ▼

Width: ▼ px ▼

Height: ▼ px ▼

5 Enter the details for the exact placement of the div tag. This can be either as pixels or as percent

Placement

Top: 50 ▼ px ▼

Right: ▼ px ▼

Bottom: ▼ px ▼

Left: 100 ▼ px ▼

Beware

Once an item has been positioned with a div tag, preview the page in your default browser, to make sure it appears as expected.

121

6 The item is added to the page, and positioned according to the properties specified in Steps 4 and 5

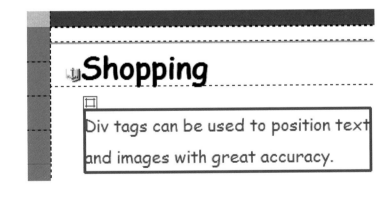

Shopping

Div tags can be used to position text and images with great accuracy.

Don't forget

Empty div tags can be inserted into a file and then have content added to them. Alternatively, content can be selected, and then have the div tag applied to it. Either way, the content will be positioned and formatted according to the properties of the inserted div tag.

7 The div tag is added to the HTML code

```
185        <p> </p>
186        <div class="position" id="position">Div tags can <br />
187   be used to position text and images with great accuracy.</div>
188   <p> </p>
```

Floating Items

Another way to position items on a page is to use the "float" option. This can be used to position items to the left or right of the page, so that other elements can then wrap around them in that position. The float option can be used on any CSS rule, but probably the best way is to use it within a div tag. To do this:

1 Add an element that you want to float left or right of the page

| Link one |
| Link two |
| Link three |
| Link four |

Text and images can be formatted with div tags.

2 Select Insert Div Tag, from the Insert panel

INSERT

Common ▼

Hyperlink
Email Link
Named Anchor
Horizontal Rule
Table
Insert Div Tag

3 Give the div tag a class name and an ID tag

Insert Div Tag

Insert: Wrap around selection ▼

Class: image_div ▼

ID: image_div ▼

New CSS Rule

OK
Cancel
Help

4 Click on the New CSS Rule button, and click OK

5 Check the settings in the New CSS Rule window (the Selector Type should be ID, and the Selector Name should be the one specified in Step 3). Click OK

6 In the CSS Rule Definition section, select the Box option

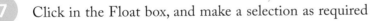

7 Click in the Float box, and make a selection as required

8 Click OK

9 The image is positioned according to the select in Step 7

Text and images can be formatted with div tags

Other CSS Properties

The other categories of properties that can be applied through the CSS Rule Definition dialog box are:

CSS Rule definition for

Category

Type
Background
Block
Box
Border
List
Positioning
Extensions

Don't forget

Background properties can be applied to items, such as text and tables, within an HTML document.

Don't forget

Block properties can be used on text, to format and position letters and words with greater flexibility than you could achieve by just using the Type category rules.

- Background. This contains properties for the background of a rule. These include background color, background image, and how a background element appears and is positioned

- Block. Properties in this category relate mainly to text spacing and alignment

- Box. In addition to specifying the position of an element within a container (box) on the page, it can also be used to specify the size and spacing of the container

- Border. This contains properties for the border of an element – for instance, the border of a table. The settings include style, width, and the color of the border

- List. This allows you to change the appearance of lists within a rule. The settings available include type of bullet, image for the bullet, and the bullet's position

- Positioning. This can be used to position an element to an exact point on a page

- Extensions. This contains properties for elements, such as page breaks for printing, the appearance of the cursor, and special effects

7 Using Hyperlinks

This chapter looks at how different types of hyperlinks can be used to link elements of a website with other pages and other sites.

About Hyperlinks

Without hyperlinks (or just links), the web would be an unconnected collection of pages and sites that would be tortuous to navigate around, since you would have to specify the web address (URL) for each page that you wanted to view. Hyperlinks simplify this process considerably: they are pieces of HTML coding that create "clickable" regions on a web page – users can click on a hyperlink, and it will take them to the linked item. In simple terms, hyperlinks are shortcuts for jumping between elements on the web.

Both text and images can be used as hyperlinks: text usually appears underlined when it is acting as a hyperlink and, for both elements, the cursor turns into a pointing hand when it is positioned over a hyperlink on a web page.

The code for a simple hyperlink, to a page within the same site structure, could look like this:

<a href="news.htm">Latest News</a>

In this example, the words "Latest News" would be underlined on the page, and, when the user clicks on them, the page "news.htm" will open.

Types of hyperlinks

There are different types of hyperlinks, depending on what they are linking to:

- Absolute links. These are links that go externally, to other pages on the web. This means that the full URL has to be inserted, so that the browser knows where to look, e.g. http://www.ineasysteps.com/

- Relative links. These are links to files within the same site structure. Such a link would appear in the following format:
<a href="main.htm">My Day</a>

- Email links. These are links to specific email addresses. These are created with the following code as the link:
<a href="mailto:nickvandome@hotmail.com">Nick Vandome</a>

Don't forget

URL stands for Uniform Resource Locator, and it refers to the unique address of every page on the web.

Don't forget

Some of the items' hyperlinks can be linked to include other pages within the same website, other locations on the same page, other websites, and email addresses.

Don't forget

For relative links, the notation "../" in a hyperlink address means move up one level in the folder hierarchy, and "/" means move down one level in the hierarchy.

Linking to Documents

Links can be created to a variety of documents, including images, sounds, and video clips, but the most common type of link is to another web page. Dreamweaver provides a number of ways to achieve this:

Using the Properties Inspector

1 Select an image or piece of text that you want to make into a link

2 Click here, and enter the URL of the page to which you want to link

Link | index.html

or

Click here to browse your hard drive for a file to link to. Once you have chosen one, click on OK (Windows) or Choose (Mac)

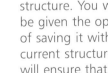

3 The selected file will now be visible in the Link box, in the Properties Inspector

Link | index.html

Beware

If you are using images as hyperlinks, make sure that they are clearly identifiable, otherwise the user may think they are just a graphical design feature.

127

Beware

If you browse to a file outside your current site structure, and then try and link to it, a warning box will appear, alerting you to the fact that the file is not contained within the current structure. You will then be given the option of saving it within the current structure. This will ensure that the link is correct.

Linking to Anchors

As well as creating hyperlinks to other pages within your own site, and external sites, it is also possible to use links to move about the same page. This can be particularly useful if you have a lot of text on a page, or several sections, and you want to enable the users to navigate around the page, without having to scroll down it too much. In Dreamweaver, this is done through the use of anchors. These are inserted on the page at the required points, and hyperlinks are then created to them from other parts of the page. To do this:

Don't forget

Anchors are also known as bookmarks, in other web authoring programs. In Dreamweaver, they are invisible elements, which means they are not seen on the published page.

1 Insert the cursor at the point where you want the anchor to appear

Hot tip

It is not necessary to select an image or a piece of text, when creating an anchor. The anchor is independent of any other item on the page, and is placed at the insertion point.

2 Select Insert, Named Anchor, from the menu bar

3 In the Named Anchor dialog box, type a name for the anchor. This is the name that will be used in the link. Click OK

Named Anchor		✕
Anchor name: Shopping		OK
		Cancel
		Help

Beware

When naming anchors, give them a single-word name. It is possible to enter more than one word in the dialog box, but this can cause problems when the link is trying to find the anchor name.

4 The anchor will be denoted on the page by this element. Click on it to see the anchor's properties

5 Select the image or piece of text on the page that is going to act as the link to the named anchor

Around Pristina

There are a lot of interesting **shopping experiences** in Pristina.

6 In the Properties Inspector, enter the name of the anchor in the Link box, preceded by the "#" symbol

Link #shopping

7 It is also possible to link to an anchor in another document, in which case, the full filename should be inserted in the Link box, followed by the "#" symbol and the anchor name as above

Link index.html#shopping

8 The linked text is denoted on the page with underlining

Around Pristina

There are a lot of interesting <u>shopping experiences</u> in Pristina.

Hot tip

If you are using a lot of anchors on a page, it is advisable to include links back to the top of the page. This means that the user will not feel lost in the middle of a long document. To include a link back to the beginning of a document, insert an anchor at the top of the page, and name it "Top". Then move further down the document and type "Top" or "Top of Page". Select the text, and create a hyperlink to "#Top". When clicked, this should then take the user to the "Top" anchor, at the beginning of the document.

Don't forget

Press F12 or select File, Preview in Browser, to test the page in a browser and to make sure that the link goes to the correct anchor.

Creating an Email Link

To create a link that allows the user to access an email address, first insert the cursor at the point where you want the link to appear; then, to create the email link:

1 Click on the Email Link button on the Insert panel

INSERT

Common ▼

🚫 Hyperlink

📧 Email Link

Hot tip

If you include an email link on your site, it is a good idea to include some form of privacy statement, saying that you will not pass on any email addresses that you receive as a result of a message that is sent to you. Unfortunately, there are some unscrupulous individuals who do this sort of thing, resulting in the people being deluged with junk email.

2 In the Email Link dialog box, insert the text that will be displayed for the link, and enter the email address to which the link will point. Click OK

Email Link

Text: Email Nick Vandome

Email: nickvandome@mac.com

OK
Cancel
Help

3 The linked text will appear on the page and, when it is selected, the email address to which it is linked will be shown in the Properties Inspector. When the link is activated in a browser, the user's email program will open, with the address pre-inserted in the To box

Email Nick Vandome

None ▼ **B** *I* ≔ ⁝⁞ ±≣ ±≣ Title

mailto:nickvandome@mac.com ▼ 🌐📁 Target

Point-to-File Links

When you are creating links, there may be times when you do not want to insert the filename of the document to which you want to link, but rather just point to a file and instruct Dreamweaver to link to that item. To do this:

 Select a piece of text, or an image. Ensure the Files panel is open and visible

 shopping experiences in Pristina.

 Beware

The Point-to-File technique cannot be used to create links to external web pages, even if they are opened next to the document window.

In the Properties Inspector, click on the HTML button

PROPERTIES
<> HTML
CSS

Don't forget

To position two files next to each other, select Window, Tile Horizontally (or Vertically), from the menu bar.

131

Click on this icon in the Properties Inspector, and drag it into the file to be linked to

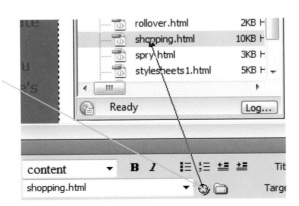

 Don't forget

The Point-to-File technique can also be used to link to an anchor point that has been inserted into a page.

Image Maps

An image map is a device that allows you to insert links to multiple files within a single image. Links within an image map are created with "hotspots", which are drawn over an image. Image maps can be used with any image that has easily identifiable areas. To create an image map:

Don't forget

Dreamweaver uses client-side image maps, which means the linked information is stored within the HTML document itself. The other type of image map is a server-side one, which contains the linking information in a separate file. In general, client-side image maps operate more quickly.

 Insert the image that is going to serve as the image map, and select it by clicking on it once

 In the Properties Inspector, click on one of the Hotspot tools

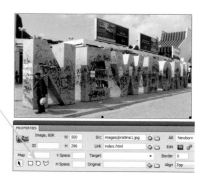

Beware

Do not overlap hotspots, or the user may have problems linking to the correct file.

Draw an area on the image that is going to act as a hotspot. This is the area that the user will be able to click on and jump to the linked file

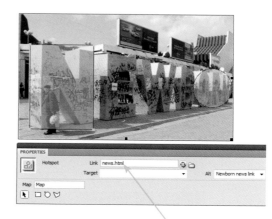

Don't forget

Click on the arrow next to the Hotspot tool, if you want to select a hotspot. This can be used to select hotspots, move them, or resize them. If you want to change a link for a hotspot, you first have to select it with this tool.

After a hotspot has been drawn, enter a file to link to here, or browse to select a file from your hard drive

8 Using Tables

This chapter shows how to create and edit tables, so that they can be used to display content on a website.

Designing with Tables

One of the biggest challenges for any web designer, is to create a page layout that is both versatile and visually appealing. This invariably involves combining text and images, and, before the advent of tables in HTML, it was a considerable problem trying to get everything in the right place. Even when elements looked correct on the designer's computer, there was no guarantee that they would appear the same when viewed on different computers, and with different browsers. However, tables changed all that.

HTML tables are one of the most important design tools available to web authors. Although their name suggests that they should perhaps only be used to collate and display figures, this is definitely not the case: tables can contain the same content as that placed at any other point on an HTML page. They can then be used to position different elements, and, since each item can be placed in its own individual cell within the table, the designer can be confident that this is the position in which they will appear, regardless of the browser used.

Tables can be used for simple formatting techniques, such as aligning text and images, or they can be used to create complex page designs:

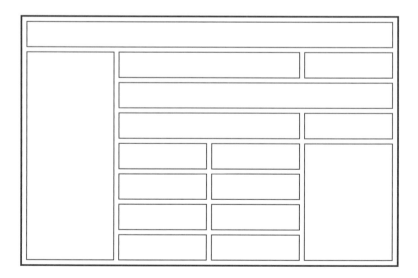

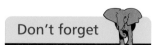

Don't forget

With the increased use of CSS for formatting HTML content, the use of tables for formatting has declined. This is because CSS can be used to position items anywhere within a web page. However, tables are still used for presenting numerical data, and they can also still be used for formatting, if required.

Don't forget

HTML tables are made up of a grid for the whole table, into which rows and cells are placed. The HTML code for these is: table – <table> </table>; row – <tr> </tr>; cell – <td> </td>.

Hot tip

If the borders of a table are made invisible, i.e. set to 0, the user will not be aware that the content on the page is inside a table. This can make complex designs look even more impressive.

Inserting a Table

You can insert as many tables as you like on a page, and tables can also be nested, i.e. tables placed within other tables. This provides even more versatility in the design process. When a table is inserted, various attributes can be set initially. However, it is also possible to edit and amend a table's attributes at any time after it has been created. To insert a table:

 Click on the Table button, on the Insert panel

Don't forget

Tables can also be created by selecting Insert, Table, from the menu bar. This brings up the same dialog box as when using the Insert panel.

Enter the number of rows and columns that are required for the table

Enter a value for the size of the table. Click here to select a percentage or a pixel size. If it is a percentage, this will be a percentage of the browser window in which it is being viewed. The pixel size is the actual, physical size of the table

Hot tip

Use the percentage setting for the width of a table, if you want to make sure it will all fit in the user's browser. However, this could affect the way some of the content is displayed within the table. Use the pixel setting, if you want the formatting to remain exactly as designed.

...cont'd

4 Enter a size for the table border. A value of 0 will create an invisible border, and the default value is 1

5 Enter values for the cell padding and the cell spacing. Cell padding affects how much space there is around each item in a cell, and cell spacing affects how much space there is between the cells in a table

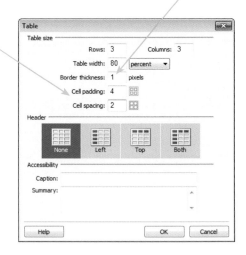

Don't forget

If the cell padding is increased, the size of the individual cells increases too, since the area for adding content in the cell is still the same, it is just the area around it that increases. If the cell spacing is increased, the size of the cells decreases, to accommodate the space around them.

6 Click OK to create the table

A table with cell padding and cell spacing both at 1

Cell spacing and	cell padding are good for
formatting	tables

A table with cell padding and cell spacing both at 10

Cell spacing and	cell padding are good for
formatting	tables

136

Adding a table header

When creating a table, it can be useful to insert a header describing its contents. This is particularly important from an accessibility point of view, i.e. for people who are blind, or partially sighted, and will be accessing the website through a device that will read the content on the page. To add a descriptive header:

1 Select one of the Header options

Table

Table size

Rows: 3   Columns: 3

Table width: 500   pixels ▼

Border thickness: 1   pixels

Cell padding: 4

Cell spacing: 2

Header

None   Left   Top   Both

Accessibility

Caption: Making tables accessible

Summary:

Help   OK   Cancel

2 Enter a description for the header

3 Click OK

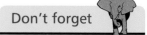

Don't forget

The header does not affect any of the other properties of the table – it will still have the same number of columns and rows.

137

4 The header is displayed in a separate row in the table

Making tables accessible

Editing a Table

If you create a table, and then decide you want to change some of its attributes, it is possible to do so through the Properties Inspector. In addition to the settings that can be used in the Insert Table dialog box, there are also some other attributes that can be used:

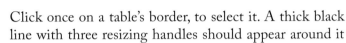

Don't forget

The resizing handles, that appear when a table is selected, can be used to change the dimensions of the table by dragging. The handle on the bottom resizes the table vertically, the one on the right side resizes it horizontally, and the one in the bottom-right corner resizes it both vertically and horizontally. Hold down Shift while dragging this handle to change the dimensions proportionally.

1 Click once on a table's border, to select it. A thick black line with three resizing handles should appear around it

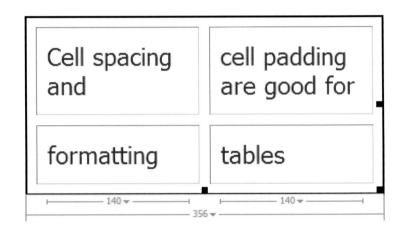

2 Once a table is selected, the Table Properties Inspector will appear:

Hot tip

It is not essential to name tables, but it is a good way to keep track of them, if you are using a lot that contain similar items of information.

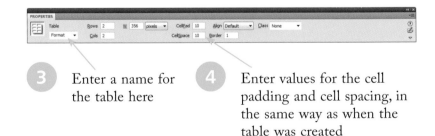

3 Enter a name for the table here

4 Enter values for the cell padding and cell spacing, in the same way as when the table was created

5 Click here to access options for aligning the table on the page: this can be Left, Center or Right

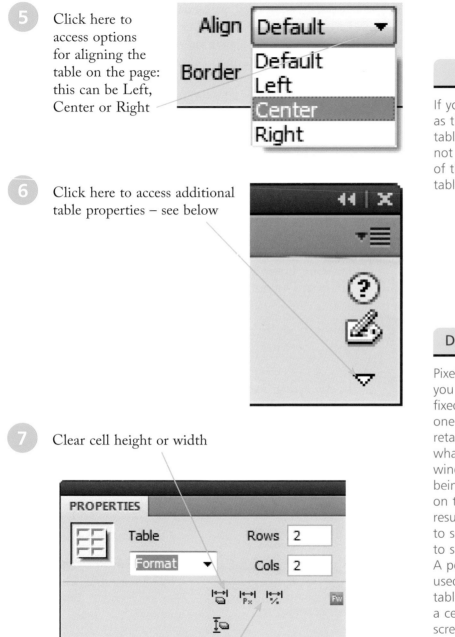

Align **Default** ▼

Default
Left
Center
Right

Border

Beware

If you select an image as the background for a table, make sure it does not detract from the rest of the content of the table itself.

6 Click here to access additional table properties – see below

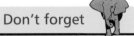

Don't forget

Pixels can be used if you want to create a fixed-width table, i.e. one where the content retains its format, whatever the size of the window in which it is being viewed. Depending on the design, this can result in the user having to scroll left and right to see the whole page. A percentage can be used if you want the table to always take up a certain portion of the screen. This can result in the content on the page becoming distorted from the original design.

7 Clear cell height or width

PROPERTIES

Table   Rows 2

Format ▼   Cols 2

8 Change the table height or width to pixels or percent

Rows and Columns

When tables are being used, particularly for complex designs, it is unlikely that the correct number of rows and columns will be specified first time. As shown on page 124, it is possible to increase or decrease the number of rows and columns by selecting the table and amending the values in the Table Properties Inspector. This can also be achieved as follows:

As shown on page 124

Don't forget

Rows and columns can also be inserted or deleted, by inserting the cursor in the table (but not selecting the table) and selecting Modify, Table, from the menu bar.

1 Insert the cursor in the table where you want to add or delete rows or columns. Right-click (Windows) or Ctrl+click (Mac), and select Table

2 Insert a single row or column by selecting Insert Row or Insert Column

Table	▸	Select Table
Paragraph Format	▸	Merge Cells
List	▸	Split Cell...
Align	▸	Insert Row
Font	▸	Insert Column
Style	▸	Insert Rows or Columns...
CSS Style		

3 To insert multiple rows or columns, click Insert Rows or Columns

4 In the dialog box, enter whether you want to insert rows or columns, the number to be inserted, and where you want them placed in relation to the insertion point

5 Click OK to insert the specified number of rows or columns

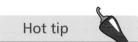

Hot tip

Rows and columns can be resized by following step 1, and then selecting Increase Row Span, Increase Column Span, Decrease Row Span, or Decrease Column Span, from the contextual menu. They can also be resized by dragging the row or column border.

Insert Rows or Columns

Insert: ◉ Rows
         ○ Columns

Number of rows: 2

Where: ○ Above the Selection
        ◉ Below the Selection

OK
Cancel
Help

140

Selecting Cells

Once a table has been created, it can be useful to select individual cells, or groups of cells, so that specific formatting options can be applied to them. For instance, you may want to have a table where the top row of cells is a different size or color from the rest of the cells in the table. Or you may want to apply separate formatting options to single cells.

Selecting cells

Insert the cursor in the cell you want to select; hold and drag to the outer border of the cell. A thick dark line appears around the cell, to indicate that it has been selected. To select more than one cell, keep dragging until all of the required cells have been covered

Click and drag to select

Merging cells

Once cells have been selected, it is then possible to merge them together, independently of the other cells in the table. This is an excellent formatting device, as it allows the designer to break the symmetrical pattern of a table, which gives increased flexibility. To merge cells once they have been selected:

1   With the required cells selected, right-click (Windows) or Ctrl+click (Mac), and select Table, Merge Cells

2   Or click here, on the Properties Inspector

3   The selected cells are now merged independently of the other cells in the table

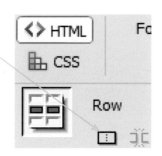

Hot tip

If the cell you are trying to select is in the first column of a table, you have to drag the cursor to the right-hand border of the cell. If it is in the last column of a table, you have to drag the cursor to the left-hand border of the cell. If the cell you are trying to select is in any other column in the table, it can be selected by dragging the cursor to the left- or right-hand border. Similarly for selecting a cell within rows in a table.

141

Hot tip

Entire rows and columns can be selected, by positioning the cursor on a border until a thick black arrow appears, and clicking once.

Don't forget

Cells can also be merged by selecting them, and then selecting Modify, Table, Merge Cells, from the menu bar.

Splitting cells

Any cell within a table can be split into smaller parts, regardless of whether it has already been merged or not. To do this:

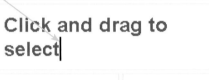

1 Insert the cursor in the cell you want to split

Beware

The Split Cell option is only available if you select a single cell. If you try and activate this command when more than one cell is selected, it will be grayed out, i.e. unavailable.

2 Right-click (Windows) or Ctrl+click (Mac), and select Table, Split Cell, from the contextual menu

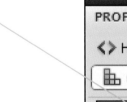

3 Or click here, on the Properties Inspector

Don't forget

If you split a cell that contains content, i.e. text or images, this will be placed in the left-hand cell, if the cell is split by columns, and the top cell, if it is split by rows.

4 In the Split Cell dialog box, select whether you want to split the cell into rows or columns, and the required number. Click OK

9 Assets

The process of creating websites can involve using the same basic designs and elements several times over. This chapter explains how to repeat commonly used items across a website, through the use of elements, in the Assets panel and Library.

Managing Assets

The Assets panel is an area that keeps track of many of the elements that you use in creating your websites. These include:

- Images
- Colors
- Hyperlinks
- Multimedia content, such as Flash and Shockwave
- Video
- Scripts
- Templates
- Library items

You do not have to add items to the Assets panel (except for templates and Library items), since all of the relevant content is automatically added to the Assets panel when it is inserted into the Dreamweaver page. There are two ways to manage Assets: either on a site-wide basis, or as Favorites, which are usually items that you want to use on several pages. To view the site assets:

Don't forget

The Assets panel will only show items for sites that have been defined. Once this has been done, the Assets panel can recognize the items in the site's cache.

Hot tip

Using the color assets is a good way to help achieve a consistent design throughout a website. Colors can easily be used on multiple pages, without you having to remember the exact one each time.

1. Select Window, Assets, from the menu bar, to access the Assets panel

2. Select the Site button, and click on the Refresh button to view the assets for the current site

Creating Favorites

Assets that are going to be used regularly, such as an image that will appear on all the pages of a site, or a hyperlink back to the home page, can be added to the Favorites list, for quick access. To do this:

Select an asset in the Site list, and click here to add it to the Favorites

or

Select an item in Design view, and right-click (Windows) or Ctrl+click (Mac) and select the relevant Add To command

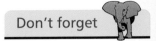

Don't forget

The Favorites list can also be used to add new assets, such as colors or hyperlinks.

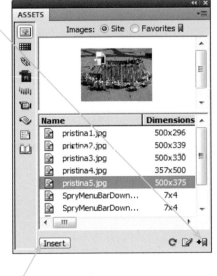

Applying assets

Assets are applied slightly differently, depending on the item:

For images, Flash, Shockwave, video, and scripts, select the item, and then click on Insert to place it on the page

For colors and links, select the relevant item in Design view; then select the asset, and click on Apply to have it take effect on the page

Don't forget

To remove an asset from the Favorites list, select it in the Favorites panel, and then click here:

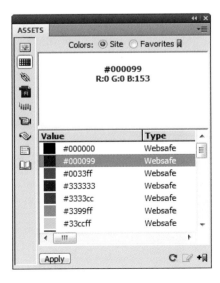

Don't forget

Assets can also be applied by dragging them from the Assets panel onto a page, in Design view.

Using Templates

Template files have been a common feature in word-processing and desktop-publishing programs for several years now. These are files that contain standard elements that recur in certain types of documents. The template can be used to store the recurring items, and new content can also be added, once a document is opened using the template as a foundation. This is an excellent device for producing a consistent design for items, such as newsletters and brochures, and it is also a time-saving device, because the basic design only has to be created once.

Recognizing the value of templates for web designers, Dreamweaver has powerful facilities for creating and using templates. This means that designers can quickly create a consistent theme for a website, while still retaining the freedom to add new content to pages.

Templates in Dreamweaver can be created from scratch, or existing files can be converted into templates. New files can then be created, based on an existing template. It is also possible to edit the content of template files.

When templates are created, you can specify which areas are constant, e.g. a company logo, and which are editable. This gives you a good degree of control over the pages that are created from your templates.

Some areas in a document created from a template remain static and cannot be edited, while others are fully editable. Editable regions are denoted by a green tag, with the name of the region.

Don't forget

When a new document is opened from a template, the document is based on the template, rather than being the template file itself. When it is first opened, the document will display the same content as the template file, but new items can then be added to the new document.

Don't forget

The colors for the tags in templates can be changed, by selecting Edit, Preferences, from the menu bar, and then selecting Highlighting and a color for each of the regions within the template file.

Insert_logo (180 x 90)	
Link one	Main Content
Link two	**Editable Content**
Link three	Non-editable content
Link four	Non-editable content
The above links demonstrate a basic navigational	

Creating Templates

Templates can be created from scratch, or existing files can be converted into templates.

Creating a new template

1 Select File, New, from the menu bar

2 Select Blank Template and a template type. Click OK

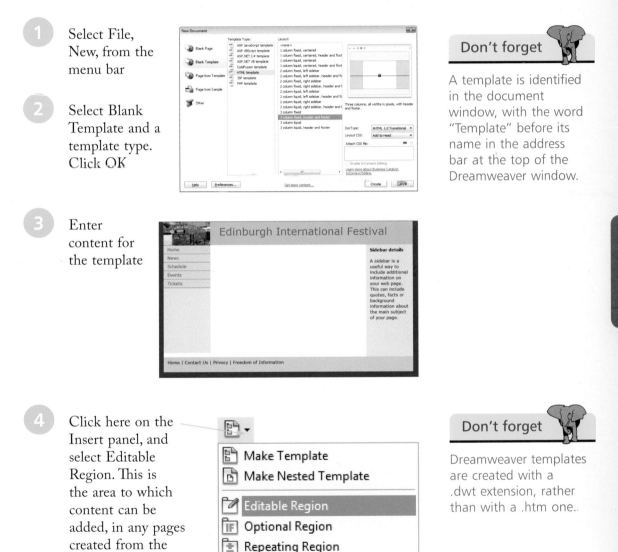

3 Enter content for the template

4 Click here on the Insert panel, and select Editable Region. This is the area to which content can be added, in any pages created from the template

147

Don't forget

A template is identified in the document window, with the word "Template" before its name in the address bar at the top of the Dreamweaver window.

Don't forget

Dreamweaver templates are created with a .dwt extension, rather than with a .htm one.

...cont'd

5 Enter a name for the editable region, and click OK

New Editable Region

Name: Main Content

This region will be editable in documents based on this template.

OK
Cancel
Help

6 The Editable Region is inserted into the template, and is indicated by this tag

Don't forget

Saved templates are placed in a Templates folder within the current site structure. This folder is created automatically by Dreamweaver, when a template is first saved.

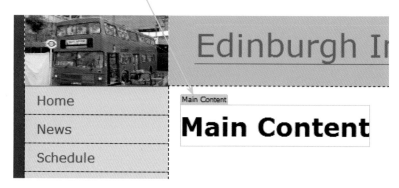

Edinburgh I

Home

News

Schedule

Main Content

Main Content

7 Select File, Save As Template, from the menu bar. Select a site for the template, and give it a name

Save As Template

Site: CS5 Website

Existing templates: (no templates)

Description:

Save as: festival1

Save
Cancel

Help

8 Click Save

Creating a template from an existing document

1 Open the document you want to use as a template

2 Click on the Editable Region button, on the Common tab on the Insert bar

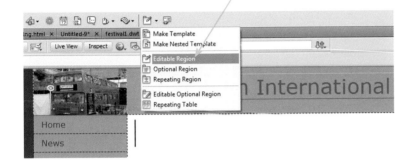

3 Since editable regions can only be inserted into templates, a message will appear, saying that the file will be converted into a template file. Click OK

Dreamweaver

Dreamweaver will automatically convert this document to a template.

☐ Don't show me this message again

OK

4 Enter a name for the new editable region

5 Click OK

6 The document is now an unsaved HTML file, with the required editable region inserted

Don't forget

When a file is saved as a template, the original is also retained. This means that you can save as many files as you like from a template, safe in the knowledge that the original version will still be intact.

7 When the file is saved, it is done so as a template, in the same way as in steps 7 and 8, on page 148

Creating Template Pages

Once templates have been created, it is then possible to produce new web pages in Dreamweaver, based on these templates. To do this:

1 Select File, New, from the menu bar, and click on Page from Template

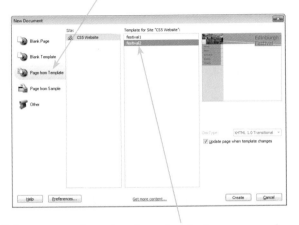

2 Select a template that has already been created, and click on Create

3 A new HTML document is opened, based on the selected template:

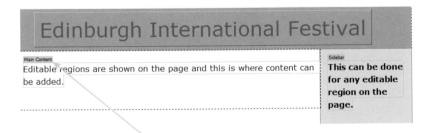

4 The editable regions are displayed on the page, and this is where content can be added

Don't forget

When templates are created, they are specific to the site in which they were produced. To use a template in another site, open it, select Save As Template, from the Menu bar, and then, in the Save As Template dialog box, select the site in which you want the template to be available.

Don't forget

In a document based on a template, the outer border identifies the template on which the document is based, and also the fact that everything within it is locked, unless it has been specified as an editable region.

Editing Templates

If you want to change the content of a particular template, this can be done by editing it. This changes the content for all of the documents that have been based on this template. So, if you have ten documents based on a single template, the size of the headings in each one could be altered by editing the heading formatting in the template file. To edit a template:

Hot tip

Templates can also be edited by right-clicking (Windows) or Ctrl+clicking (Mac) in a document based on a template and selecting Templates, Open Attached Template, from the menu that appears.

152

Don't forget

If you are updating a template, check all of the files to which it is linked, to make sure that you want to make the change to all of them. If you do not, you can detach any of the files from the template by opening it and selecting Modify, Templates, Detach from Template, from the menu bar.

1 Access the Assets panel, by selecting Window, Assets, from the menu bar

2 Click here to access the templates

3 Double-click on a template to open it

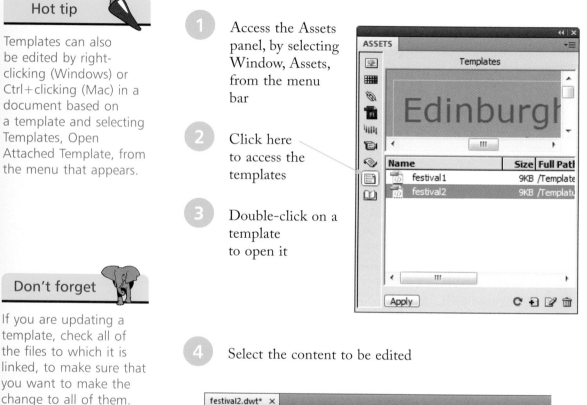

4 Select the content to be edited

5 Edit the content of the template, and select File, Save, from the menu bar

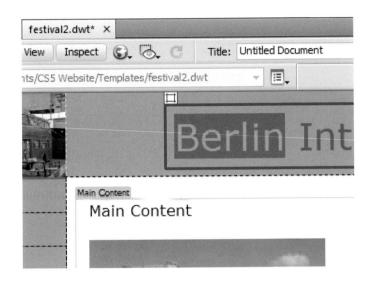

6 A dialog box will appear, asking if you want to update all the documents based on this template. If you do, select Update

Update Template Files

Update all files based on this template?

festival\festival1.html
festival\festival2.html
festival\festival3.html
festival\festival4.html
festival\festival5.html
festival\festival6.html
festival\festival7.html
festival\festival8.html
festival\festival9.html
festival\festival10.html

Update

Don't Update

...cont'd

7   The Update Pages dialog box indicates when the update
    has been completed. Click Close once this has been done

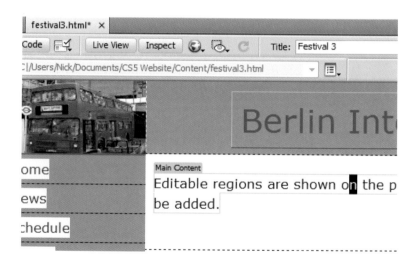

8   The changes are made to all of the affected pages

9   If they are open, save all of the individual pages that have
    been updated

About the Library

During the design process of a website, there will probably be some elements that you will want to reuse on different pages within the site. These could be static elements that appear on several pages, such as a company logo, or items where one part is updated regularly, such as a "latest news" section. Instead of having to create or insert these elements from their source locations each time you want to use them, Dreamweaver has a facility for storing them, and then dragging them onto a page whenever they are required. The location they are stored in is known as the Library. Each site can have its own individual Library, with items that are used throughout that site.

When an item is placed in the Library, it creates a Library item file that links to the source location in which that item is stored. So, if the item is an image, there will be a link to its location on the hard drive. This means that the image can be reused numerous times, without increasing the file size of the page. Rather than placing a copy of the item on a page each time it is taken from the Library, Dreamweaver creates a reference (or instance) back to the source location of the item. As long as the item is not moved from its source location, the Library version can be reused as many times as you like. Also, Library items can be updated, if required, and any changes made to them will be reflected in all of the instances of them in the site. To access the Library:

Hot tip

Before Library items can be created, the page from which they are being created has to be saved and placed within an existing site structure.

155

Click here on the
Assets panel

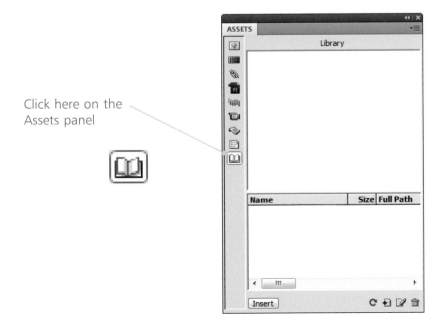

Creating Library Items

Items can be added to the Library from any open Dreamweaver document. These will then be available, in the Library, to all other pages within that site. To add items to the Library:

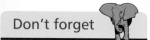
Don't forget

Blocks of text and images can be converted into Library items, as can tables, forms, and other elements, such as Flash movies.

1 Open a file in Design view and make sure the Library panel is visible, as shown on the previous page

2 Select the item that you want to include in the Library

Around Pristina

Don't forget

Images can be selected by clicking on them once, and text can be selected by dragging the cursor over the required section.

156

3 Drag and drop the item into either panel of the Library

4 Type a name for the Library item

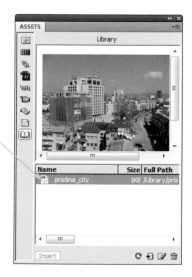

Don't forget

Items can also be added to the Library by selecting them and selecting Modify, Library, Add Object to Library, from the menu bar, or by clicking on the New Library Item button on the Assets panel.

Adding Library Items

Once items have been created in the Library, they can then be reused on any page within the site structure. To do this:

Don't forget

Library items are created as individual files, with a .lib extension.

1 Select an item in the Library

2 Drag and drop the selected Library item onto the Design-view page

or

Click on the Insert button on the Library panel

Around Pristina

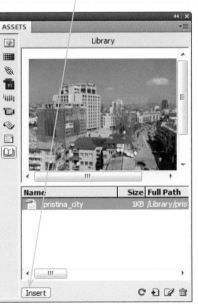

Don't forget

Once a Library item has been added to a document, it will remain there, even if it is subsequently deleted from the Library.

157

3 An instance of the Library item placed on the page. This is locked, i.e. it cannot be edited within the document itself

Don't forget

To change the color used to highlight Library items, when they are placed in a document, select Edit, Preferences, from the menu bar, select Highlighting as the category, and select a color from the box next to Library Items.

Editing Library Items

Library items are very versatile, in that it is possible to edit them in the Library itself, in which case, the changes apply to all of the instances of these items throughout the site, or individual Library items in a document can be made editable, so that they can then be edited independently.

Editing items in the Library

If you open and edit an item in the Library itself, these changes can be applied to all occurrences of that item throughout a whole site. To do this:

Don't forget

When a Library item is opened, it is done so in a separate window, with the words "Library Item" in the title.

Don't forget

A Library item can also be edited, by clicking on the arrow at the top of the Assets panel and selecting Edit.

1. Open an item in the Library by double-clicking the name,
   or by selecting it and clicking the Edit button

2. In the Library Item window, make editing changes to the item. Select File, Save, from the menu bar, to apply the changes

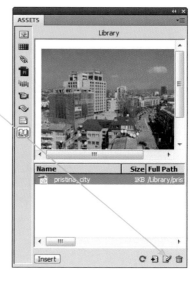

3. The Update Library Items dialog box will appear. If you want to update this item in all of the files it occurs in, click Update

Editing Library items in a document

After a Library item has been placed in a document, it is still possible to perform certain editing tasks on it:

1 Select a Library item on a document page by clicking on it once. It will not be possible to edit this directly

Home | News | Shopping | Entertainment

`12> <a> <mm:libitem>`

Src /Library/Nav_bar.lbi   [Open]   [Detach from original]
[Recreate]

2 The Library Properties box will be displayed

Click "Detach from original" to detach the item in the document from the source Library item. This means that it can be edited in the document window, but it will not have any changes applied to it if the source Library item is edited

Src /Library/Nav_bar.lbi   [Open]   [Detach from original]
[Recreate]

Click Open to open the item in the Library window. The content can then be edited

Click Recreate to recreate a Library item, if the original has been deleted from the Library palette

Beware

If an instance of a Library item is detached from the source document, then it loses all of the attributes it had previously. It no longer functions as a Library item, and will not be updated if the original Library item is edited.

Editable Navigation Bars

A navigation bar is a set of buttons that can help the user navigate between the most commonly used areas, or pages of a website. They can appear at the top or the side of all pages throughout a site. This has the advantage of creating a uniform style, and it makes the user feel comfortable within the site. For information about creating navigation bars, see Chapter 7, page 118. One of the possible drawbacks with navigation bars is that if you have them throughout your site, and then decide to update a link within them, it can be a laborious task. This can be greatly simplified by creating the navigation bar as a Library item:

Hot tip

If you have a site that contains a navigation bar on several hundred pages, you will soon come to appreciate the importance of creating it as a Library item, so that it can be updated site-wide in a single operation.

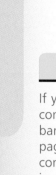

Beware

After updating a Library item, make sure that all of the relevant files are uploaded to the remote site, i.e. the one that is hosting the website.

1 Create a navigation bar, and convert it into a Library item by dragging it into one of the Library panels

2 Click here to edit the navigation bar

3 Apply the editing, and select File, Save, from the menu bar

4 You will be prompted as to whether you want to update all of the pages that contain this Library item. Click Update

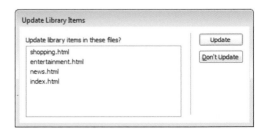

10 Advanced Features

This chapter looks at some of the more advanced features in Dreamweaver, such as forms, video, and mobile devices, and shows how they can be used to create high-quality, professional sites.

Forms

An HTML form is a set of objects that the user can interact with, to send various pieces of information to the server hosting the web page, or directly to the author of the page, which requires a piece of computer programming called a script. This can collate the information from the form, analyze it, and send it to a specified location. This can be done with a variety of scripting languages, such as Perl or Javascript. The script can either be placed within the form itself (client-side), or on the server that will be processing the information (server-side). If it is a server-side application, this is usually handled with a Common Gateway Interface script.

A form can be made up of several different elements, all of which are contained in an overall form container. Attributes and properties can then be assigned to each element, within the form structure. To create a form and set its properties:

Hot tip

If your website contains forms and is going to be published by your Internet service provider (ISP), check to make sure that they can process forms, and also for any special requirements they need included in the form.

Don't forget

Common Gateway Interface (CGI) scripts are usually written in computer languages, such as Perl, C, or Java. This is not something that can be picked up in a couple of days. There are a number of sites on the Web that offer information about CGIs, including some scripts that can be downloaded and used. One site to look at is: www.cgi-resources.com.

 Click the Forms tab on the Insert panel

The properties for a form are entered in the Form Properties Inspector, and they are:

- Form ID. This is a unique identifier for the form

- Action. If the form is being processed by a server-side script, enter the URL of the script here

- Method. This is the way information is sent to the server. The options are Get, Post, and Default

- Enctype. The type of encryption used if the form needs to be secure, e.g. if it deals with financial transactions

Form elements

There are a variety of elements that can be added to forms, and these are accessed from the Forms tab on the Insert panel. The available options are:

- Text Field. This can be used to enter single lines of data, multiple lines of data, or passwords

- Hidden Field. This can be inserted into a form to capture information about the user, or the form itself

- Textarea. Similar to a text field, except that it contains scroll bars, so that unlimited text can be entered

- Checkbox. This can be used with a list of options that the user has to select, as required. In a list of check boxes, numerous items can be selected: it is not an either/or option

- Radio Button. These are similar to check boxes, except that they only allow for a single option to be selected

- Radio Group. This allows for groups of radio buttons to be inserted, with each group containing a different option

- List/Menu. Creates a drop-down list or menu

- Jump Menu. Creates a drop-down menu, with items that contain a hyperlink to another page or object

- Image Field. This can be used to insert an image into a form, generally for design purposes

- File Field. This allows the user to select a file from their hard drive and enter it into the form

- Button. This can be used to insert Submit or Reset buttons

- Label. This is an optional button that can be used to give textual labels to form elements

- Fieldset. This is a container for a group of related form elements

- Spry elements. These are Spry elements that can be used within a form. For more information on Spry elements, see pages 169–171

Hot tip

A form has a non-printing border that can be used to help format items within the form. If this is not visible when the form is inserted, select View, Visual Aids, Invisible Elements, from the menu bar.

Hot tip

Forms take on the background color of the page on which they are created. However, text and images can be formatted independently within a form. Tables can also be inserted within a form, and so can the form elements placed inside them, for formatting purposes.

Frames

Traditionally, frames have had an uneasy relationship with the Web, primarily for two reasons:

- They can cause problems for older browsers, and they can also cause problems for search engines

- They are one of the harder concepts for web designers to master, particularly those new to this medium

The basic concept of frames is that the content of two or more pages is displayed on screen at the same time. Each page is known as a frame, and numerous frames can be displayed at the same time. Each frame acts independently of the others that are being displayed; so it is possible to scroll through the contents of one frame, while all of the others remain static. The final part of the frames equation is the frameset. This is the document that contains all of the frames that are being viewed. So, if there are two frames on a page, this involves three documents: the two frame pages and the frameset. The frameset is a separate HTML document that has no visible content of its own. Instead, it contains a command for the browser to display the frames that it specifies. It can also contain other details of how to display the frames.

To create frames and framesets:

164

Beware

If possible, try and avoid using frames for creating websites. Instead, use templates to create a consistent look for sites.

1. Select File, New, from the menu bar

2. Select Page from Sample, and click on Framesets. Select the required design. Click Create

3. The selected style opens in the document window

4 The Properties Inspector displays the currently selected frame

5 Add content by clicking in each frame and adding

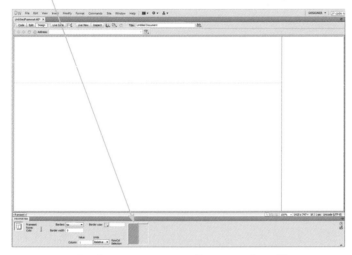

content in the same way as for any other file

6 Drag the frame borders to change their sizes

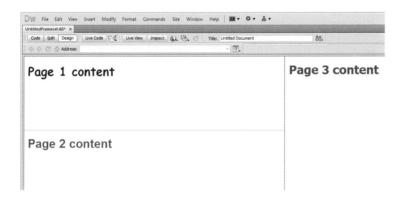

Page 1 content

Page 3 content

Page 2 content

Hot tip

If some content is not visible in a frame, the frame's borders can be resized by dragging them (see next page).

...cont'd

7 Once content has been added to each frame, select File, Save All, from the menu bar

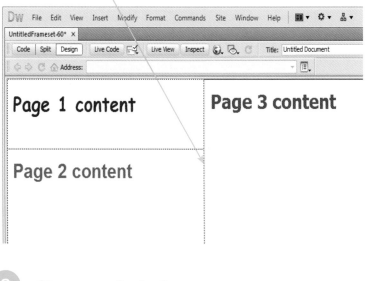

Don't forget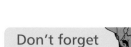

Each frame can be given a unique name in the Properties Inspector. This can be useful when adding hyperlinks between frames.

8 Give a name for the frameset, and click Save

File name: UntitledFrameset-60

Beware

Hyperlinks can be added to frames in the same way as to other HTML files. However, to make sure they open up in the correct location, use the Target box in the Properties Inspector. This will let you select a specific location for where the linked file opens. Some practice is required when working with links in frames.

9 Give each individual frame a name and click Save. You will be prompted to save each frame, until all of the elements of the frameset have been saved

Save

File name: UntitledFrame-3

Video

it is now a common occurrence to see video on websites, and a generation of users are coming to expect this feature. A common video format is Flash Video (FLV), as it can be successfully compressed and played on a variety of browsers without the need for video player plug-ins. To insert Flash Video:

1. In the Insert panel, select Media, FLV

2. The Insert FLV window has options for selecting and formatting video

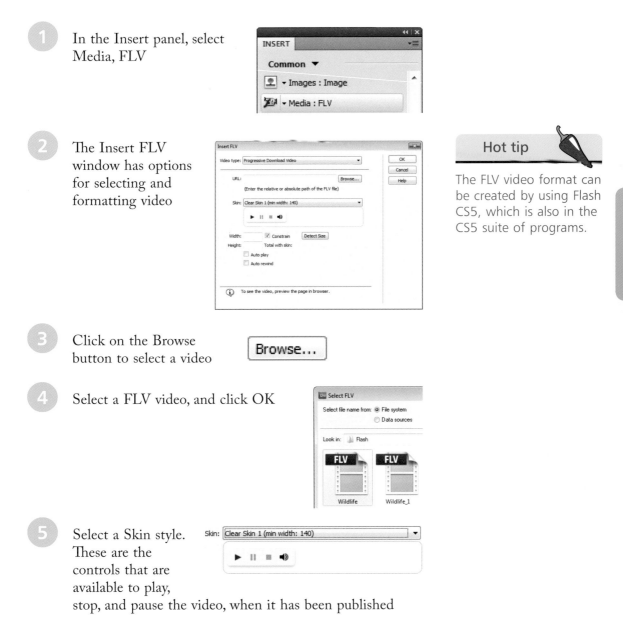

Hot tip

The FLV video format can be created by using Flash CS5, which is also in the CS5 suite of programs.

3. Click on the Browse button to select a video

4. Select a FLV video, and click OK

5. Select a Skin style. These are the controls that are available to play, stop, and pause the video, when it has been published

167

6 Enter the size at which you would like the video to appear on your page. Click on the Detect Size button, to set the size to that of the original video file

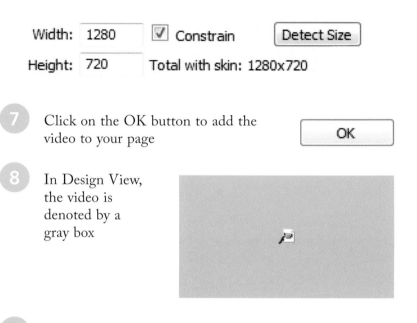

7 Click on the OK button to add the video to your page

8 In Design View, the video is denoted by a gray box

9 Click on the video box to show the Properties Inspector. These properties are similar to those selected in the Insert FLV window

10 The video, and Skin option, can be previewed in Live View

Spry Elements

Any user of the Web knows that there are a lot of impressive and sophisticated effects that can be included within web pages. A lot of these effects require complicated coding, which is too daunting for many designers. However, in Dreamweaver CS5, there is a set of tools that can create these types of effects using a graphical interface. This is known as the Spry Framework.

The Spry Framework is a library of items, created in Javascript code, that can be inserted into pages within Dreamweaver, to create effects, such as sophisticated menu bars, tabbed panels, and text-validation fields.

There are several Spry elements that can be used, but the process is similar for all of them:

Don't forget

The full name for the Spry elements in Dreamweaver is Spry Framework for Ajax.

1. Click on the Spry tab on the Insert panel, and select one of the elements

2. The selected item is added to the Dreamweaver page

3. Each Spry effect has CSS style sheets attached to it, and these are automatically added to the CSS Styles panel

Don't forget

Completed Spry elements are a combination of HTML, CSS, and Javascript code.

...cont'd

④ A SpryAssets folder is created, containing all of the code that is required for the Spry item

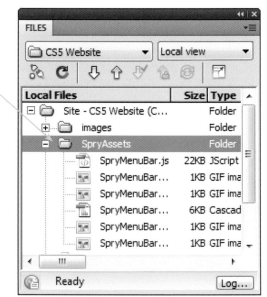

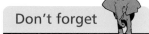

Don't forget

The SpryAssets folder is created automatically, once a Spry element has been added to a page, and the page has been saved.

⑤ When the Spry item is previewed in a browser, its full functionality is displayed

Beware

While Spry elements can be added visually to a Dreamweaver page, the code that is used to create them can be considerably more complicated.

Spry Widgets

Spry widgets are a collection of items that can add sophisticated functionality to a web page. This example is for a menu bar.

Spry Menu Bar

This widget creates drop-down menus:

171

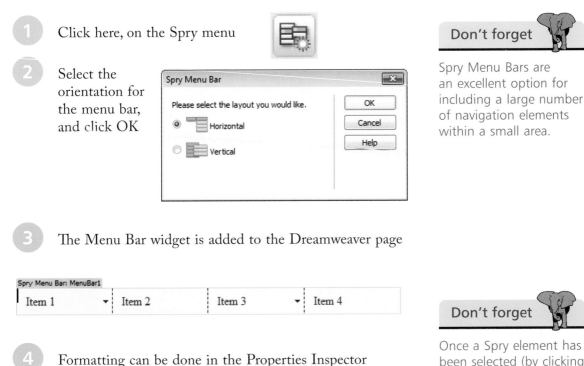

1 Click here, on the Spry menu

2 Select the orientation for the menu bar, and click OK

3 The Menu Bar widget is added to the Dreamweaver page

4 Formatting can be done in the Properties Inspector

5 Preview the Menu Bar in Live View, to see its operation

Don't forget

Spry Menu Bars are an excellent option for including a large number of navigation elements within a small area.

Don't forget

Once a Spry element has been selected (by clicking on the colored tab at the top of the element), the Properties Inspector displays the formatting options for that item.

Behaviors

Behaviors in Dreamweaver are pre-programmed events that are triggered by the user performing a certain action on the page. For instance, the action of rolling the cursor over an image could trigger the event of a sound being played. Behaviors are created by Javascript programming, but Dreamweaver contains several pre-written behaviors that can be inserted into a page, using the Behaviors Inspector.

Creating a behavior consists of two parts, defining the action that is going to be performed, and stating the event that will be triggered by the action. There are several events that can be selected, and more can be downloaded from the Web. When an event is selected, the action to trigger it is automatically included. To create a behavior:

Don't forget

All browsers handle behaviors differently. In the Behaviors panel, it is possible to specify the version of the browser for which you are creating the behavior.

Hot tip

If you want to attach a behavior to a whole page, create it without selecting anything within the document. This behavior is usually triggered when the file is opened on the Web, and is identified by the onLoad event.

172

1   Select an item to which you want to attach a behavior, such as an image

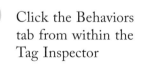

2   Click the Behaviors tab from within the Tag Inspector

Don't forget

The script for behaviors is inserted into the head portion of the HTML source code. If you know Javascript, you can write your own scripts and include them as behaviors.

3 Click here to access the Actions menu. Select the action that you want to use for the selected item

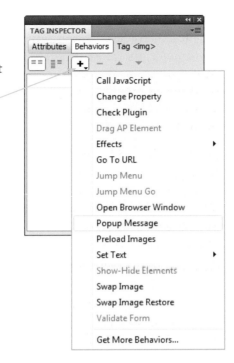

Don't forget

The events associated with selected images, text, or hyperlinks include: onMouseOver, which is when the cursor is moved over the selected item; onMouseOut, which is when the cursor is moved off the selected item; and onClick, which is when the selected item is clicked.

4 The action is entered, and the default event (the one that will trigger the action) is inserted. Here it is onMouseOver, which means the action will be triggered when the cursor is rolled over the selected item

173

Javascript

In Dreamweaver, some effects, such as rollover buttons, are created using a programming language called Javascript. This is a popular language for use on the Web, and it can be inserted into web pages for a variety of purposes, such as producing scrolling text or dates that update themselves automatically. If you are proficient in writing Javascript, it is possible to write and insert this code yourself. (It is also possible to include other scripting languages, such as VBScript.) To insert Javascript into a Dreamweaver page:

Don't forget

Scripts can be entered while you are working in Design view or Code view, or a combination of both.

1 Click the Script button on the HTML tab on the Insert panel

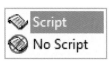

2 Click Script, to select the type of script to write

> Script
> No Script

3 In the Content box, enter your script

Hot tip

To learn Javascript, look at "Javascript in Easy Steps" in this series.

Script

Type: text/javascript
Source:
Content: linearTransition: function(time, begin, change, d
{
        if (time > duration) return ch
        return begin + (time / duratic
},
sinusoidalTransition: function(time, be
{

No script:

OK
Cancel
Help

Don't forget

For an in-depth look at Javascript and Dreamweaver, select Help, Dreamweaver Help, from the menu bar, and select Javascript from the index, or enter it into the search box.

4 Click OK, to insert the script into a file

Designing for Mobile Devices

As web users become more and more sophisticated, they are looking to have their content delivered in a variety of different ways, particularly to mobile devices, such as cellphones and personal digital assistants (PDAs). This presents a considerable challenge for designers, as they have to be aware that users may be looking at their content on devices that have considerably smaller screens than standard computers. It is, therefore, useful to be able to see how content designed in Dreamweaver will appear on mobile devices. This can be done with a feature known as Device Central. To use this:

Don't forget

Files have to be saved before they can be previewed in the Device Central environment.

 Open or create a Dreamweaver file. Click here, on the Document toolbar, and select Preview in Device Central

Title:	Untitled Document
Preview in IExplore	F12
Preview in Device Central	Ctrl+Alt+F12
Preview in Adobe BrowserLab	Ctrl+Shift+F12
Edit Browser List...	

 The content is displayed on a sample device

...cont'd

3 Click here to select specific devices on which to preview the content

Don't forget

If you are designing pages for mobile devices, preview them regularly in Device Central, so that you always know what the design will look like.

4 Click on a specific device to see the technical details

5 Depending on how the previewed content appears, it can, if necessary, then be edited in Dreamweaver, to make it display more effectively on specific mobile devices

11 Publishing

This chapter shows how to publish a site. It also explains how to work with files once a site has been published and is live.

Site Management

The final step, before publishing a site, is to check it thoroughly, to make sure that everything is working properly. This involves making sure all of the links work, and that everything looks the way it should. One way to do this is to preview the site in a browser and go through all of the pages. This can be done by pressing F12, or by selecting File, Preview in Browser. Another option is to check all of the hyperlinks in the site window. This will generate a list of all of the broken links in your site, and you can then take remedial action. To check the accuracy of the links in your entire site:

Don't forget

The functionality of a site can also be checked by accessing Live View.

Don't forget

The Check Links Sitewide command also reveals files that are orphaned, i.e. ones that do not have any links going to them from other pages. This means that it will not be possible to access them from anywhere else on the site. It also shows external links, i.e. ones that link to files outside the current site structure.

178

1 In the Files panel, select the site that you want to check, by clicking here

2 Click the Files panel menu, and select Site, Check Links Sitewide, from the Site-panel menu bar

| SEARCH | REFERENCE | VALIDATION | BROWSER COMPATIBILITY | LINK CHECKER | SITE REPORTS | FTP LOG | SERVER DEBUG |

Show: Broken Links ▾ (links to files not found on local disk)

Files	Broken Links
/entertainment.html	index.html#shopping
/index.html	shoppin .html
/news.html	index.html#shopping
/shopping.html	index.html#shopping
/festival/festival1.html	/Library/Nav Bar.lbi
/festival/festival10.html	/Library/Nav Bar.lbi

42 Total, 29 HTML, 11 Orphaned 211 All links, 192 OK, 16 Broken, 3 External

3 If there are any broken links in your site, they will be listed in the Link Checker panel

Beware

Broken links occur when the destination of a hyperlink is changed. This can happen for several reasons, such as the file's location being changed within the site structure, or the filename being changed. If you rename or move files, try to update the relevant hyperlinks as well.

Uploading a Site

Once you have checked your site structure, and made sure that there are no broken links on a site, it is time to upload it onto the server that is going to be hosting the site. If you are working on an internal intranet, then the server will probably be part of your local network, and the IT systems administrator will be able to advise you about the procedure for uploading a website. If your site is being hosted on the Internet by your Internet Service Provider (ISP), you will have to obtain the relevant settings needed when a website is being uploaded from them.

The process of uploading, or publishing, a website in Dreamweaver consists of creating an exact copy of all of the items within your local site structure on the remote server. This includes all of the HTML files, images, and other elements that have been included in your site. The same site structure is also retained, so that all of the links in your site will match their target destinations, and so will work properly.

To upload a site

1   Select Site, Manage Sites, from the menu bar

2   In the Manage Sites dialog box, select a site, and select Edit

Manage Sites

CS5 Website

New...

Edit...

Duplicate

Remove

Export...

Import...

Done   Help

Hot tip

A lot of ISPs have online advice about uploading your own website, and the settings that will be required. Try looking under their "Help" or "Technical Support" links. If possible, try to avoid telephoning, since a lot of ISPs charge premium rates for calls to their helplines. Emailing could be a useful compromise, if you do not want to telephone.

Don't forget

When you upload a site to an FTP server, the ISP hosting the site will assign it a web address (URL). This will probably be based on your own username.

...cont'd

③ In the Site Setup window, click on the Servers link

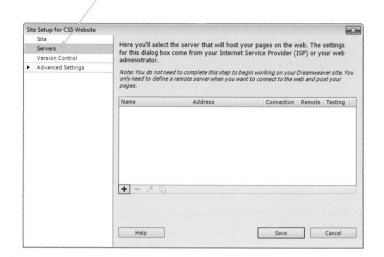

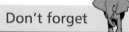

Don't forget

You will have to get the exact FTP settings from the ISP that is going to be hosting your site. In general terms, the details that are needed are:

• FTP host. This is the name for identifying the host computer system on the Internet. It is not the same as a web address (URL), or an email address

• Host directory. This is the location on the host's server where your site will be stored

• Login. This is the login name you will use to access your site's files

• Password. This is the password that you will use to access your site's files

④ Click on the Plus button, to add a new remote site

⑤ In the Basic section of the Site Setup window, enter details for the FTP host, the host directory, the login, and the password. (Not all ISPs require host-directory data, as these are assigned automatically). When this has been done, click Save

6 In the Manage Sites dialog box, click Done

7 The following message may appear, to create the site cache. Click OK

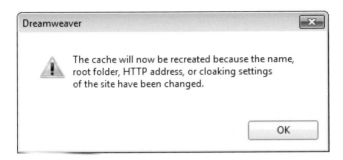

Dreamweaver

⚠ The cache will now be recreated because the name, root folder, HTTP address, or cloaking settings of the site have been changed.

OK

8 Select the root folder and click the Put button. If the site has been uploaded successfully, the remote folder should be visible in the Remote Site panel, and contain a mirror image of the local site

FILES

Show: CS5 Website

Remote Server	Size	Type	Modified	Local Files	Size	Type	Modified	Checked (
C:\Users\Nick\Documents\Server\				Site - CS5 Website (C...		Folder	31/05/2010 2:08 PM	-
festival		Folder	31/05/2010 2	festival		Folder	31/05/2010 2:08 PM	-
images		Folder	31/05/2010 2	images		Folder	31/05/2010 10:5...	-
Library		Folder	31/05/2010 2	Library		Folder	31/05/2010 2:08 PM	-
SpryAssets		Folder	31/05/2010 2	SpryAssets		Folder	31/05/2010 2:08 PM	-
Templates		Folder	31/05/2010 2	Templates		Folder	31/05/2010 2:08 PM	-
entertainment.html	14KB	HTML Do...	31/05/2010 1	entertainment.html	14KB	HTML Do...	31/05/2010 11:2...	
index.html	11KB	HTML Do...	31/05/2010 1	index.html	11KB	HTML Do...	31/05/2010 1:42 PM	
news.html	14KB	HTML Do...	31/05/2010 2	news.html	14KB	HTML Do...	31/05/2010 2:08 PM	
shopping.html	14KB	HTML Do...	31/05/2010 1	shopping.html	14KB	HTML Do...	31/05/2010 11:2...	
spry.html	3KB	HTML Do...	30/05/2010 7	spry.html	3KB	HTML Do...	30/05/2010 7:37 PM	
tables.html	2KB	HTML Do...	31/05/2010 1	tables.html	2KB	HTML Do...	31/05/2010 11:0...	

Date: 31/05/2010 2:08 PM

Log...

Beware

The Connect button is grayed out, i.e. not available, if the FTP settings have not been entered. However, when it becomes available, this is no guarantee that the FTP settings have been entered correctly.

Beware

If you have a lot of images in your site structure, or a few large ones, then your site will take longer to upload to the FTP server than if they were not there. This will give you some idea of how long users will have to wait for certain items to download.

181

Don't forget

If you experience problems when you try and upload a site with FTP, select View, Site FTP Log, from the Site-panel menu bar. This may give you some indication of the problem.

Checking Files In and Out

If you are working on a corporate website, or an intranet, it is likely that you will not be the only person working on the files that are in the site structure. If this is the case, it is important to know who is working on a certain file at a particular time. This avoids any duplication of work, and ensures that the correct version of a file is uploaded to the live site.

Dreamweaver uses a system to ensure that only one person can be working on a file at any one time, no matter how many other people there are in the team of web designers. This is known as checking files in and out. For this to work properly, it has to be activated, and then individuals can check files in and out as required.

Enabling checking in and out

Beware

If file checking in and out is not used, then it is possible for more than one person to be working on a file at the same time, if it is in a shared environment. Unless you are the sole author of a website, it is recommended that file checking in and out is turned on.

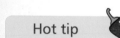

Hot tip

When the "Enable file check out" box is checked, this activates another option, one for adding the name that you want to use as identification when you are checking files in and out. Make sure it is something that the rest of the design team will recognize easily.

1. Select Site, Manage Sites, from the menu bar

2. In the Manage Sites dialog box, select the required site and click Edit

3. In the Site Setup Window, click on the Servers link

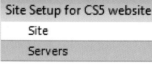

4. Click on the Edit button

5. Click on the Advanced button

6. Check on the "Enable file check-out" box

7. Click Save

Getting and Putting Files

If you want to edit a file on your site, you can do so by either opening it in the document window and then uploading it to the remote site once the changes have been made, or by opening it from the remote site itself and then making the changes. This involves using the Put and Get commands: Put transfers files from the local folder to the remote server, and Get does the reverse.

Putting files

If a file has been edited and updated, the Put command can be used to place it on the remote server:

1   In the Files panel, select the file in the local folder by clicking on it once

2   Click the Put button. Dreamweaver will connect to the remote network, and place the file in the remote folder

Getting files

1   In the Files panel, click here and select the Remote Server

2   Select a file or a folder and click the Get button, to get the selected item from the remote site

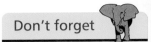

As with most publishing operations, you require an Internet connection to be able to perform the Put and Get actions, if you are connecting to a remote server, rather than a local network.

Once a connection has been made to the remote server, the Connect button changes into a Disconnect one. This indicates that you are online, and connected to the remote server. To close the connection, click on the Disconnect button. This will disconnect you from the FTP server, but will not necessarily close your ISP connection. This will probably have to be closed down in the usual way.

Individual files can be uploaded by selecting them in the Files panel and clicking the Put button, or from either Design view or Code view, by clicking on the Get/Put button on the Document toolbar.

Cloaking

Cloaking is a publishing device that can be used to prevent certain folders or file types being published. This can be useful if you are working on some draft pages, or if you want to exclude certain large file types from being published every time you update a site. To use cloaking:

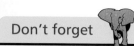

Don't forget

If you want to cloak specific files, you have to do this by cloaking the file type in the Site Definition dialog box. This could cause problems if, for instance, you wanted to cloak an HTML file, as all of the other HTML files in the site would also be cloaked. If you do want to cloak specific files, place them in a new folder, and apply cloaking to the folder.

Hot tip

If you want to specify more than one file type to be cloaked, separate the different types with a single space, in the "Cloak files ending with" box. Do not use a comma or a semicolon.

Beware

Cloaked items are excluded from site-management tasks, such as synchronizing, updating templates, and Library items. However, these functions can still be performed by selecting the folder or file individually, as this overrides any cloaking commands.

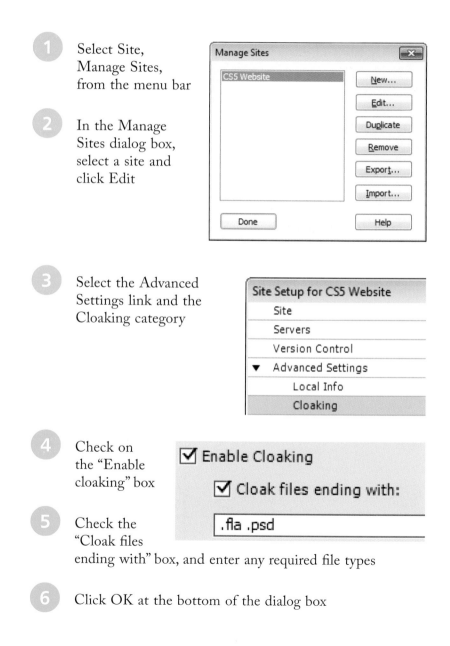

1. Select Site, Manage Sites, from the menu bar

2. In the Manage Sites dialog box, select a site and click Edit

3. Select the Advanced Settings link and the Cloaking category

4. Check on the "Enable cloaking" box

5. Check the "Cloak files ending with" box, and enter any required file types

6. Click OK at the bottom of the dialog box

Applying cloaking

Cloaking can be applied to folders, but not to individual files
(these have to be cloaked by applying a file type to be cloaked, in
the Site Definition dialog box, as shown on the previous page). To
cloak folders:

1 Select a folder in
the Files panel

2 Click here, to
access the Files-
panel menu

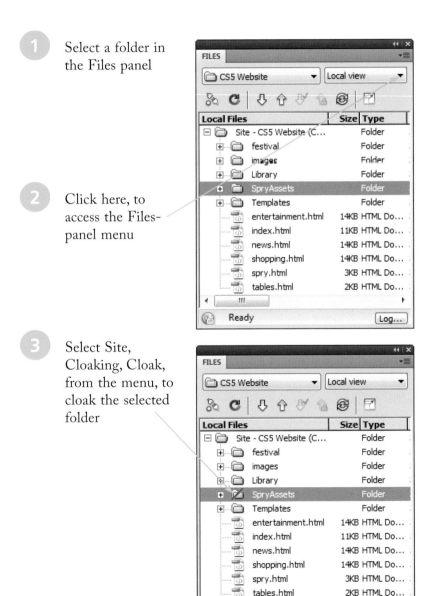

3 Select Site,
Cloaking, Cloak,
from the menu, to
cloak the selected
folder

Beware

If you are developing
draft sites, make sure
they are cloaked when
you are publishing other
files and folders.

Don't forget

Once a folder or file type
has been cloaked, a red
line is placed through it
in the Site panel.

Don't forget

Cloaked items can be
uncloaked by selecting
them in the Site panel
and selecting Cloaking,
Uncloak, from the Site-
panel menu.

Synchronizing Files

When you are updating and editing files, and checking them in and out, it is easy to lose track of whether the most recent version of a file is in the local folder, or on the remote site. Dreamweaver offers a solution to this problem, in the form of file synchronization. This automatically updates both the local and remote sites, so that the most recent version of all the site files is placed in each location. To synchronize files between the local and remote sites:

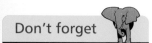

Don't forget

If you only want to synchronize certain files, select them first, in the local or the remote folder, and then select Selected Local Files Only, in the Synchronize menu of the Synchronize Files dialog box.

Don't forget

Once the synchronization options have been selected, Dreamweaver connects to the remote site, to check the versions of the files there. Therefore, make sure your Internet connection is active when you want to perform any synchronization.

Don't forget

If the latest versions of all files are in both the remote and the local site folders, then a message will appear stating this, and saying that nothing requires synchronization.

1 In the Files panel, select Site, Synchronize, from the menu bar

2 In the Synchronize Files dialog box, select whether you want to synchronize the entire site, or only the files in the local site

Synchronize Files

Synchronize: Selected Local Files Only ▼   Preview...

Direction: Put newer files to remote ▼   Cancel

☐ Delete remote files not on local drive   Help

3 Click Preview to see the files that will be updated

Synchronize

Files: 5 will be updated

Action	File	Status
⬆ Put	Library\Nav_bar.lbi	
⬆ Put	entertainment.html	
⬆ Put	index.html	
⬆ Put	news.html	
⬆ Put	shopping.html	

☐ Show all files

To change an action, select a file and click one of the icons below before clicking OK.

⬇ ⬆ 🗑 ⊘ 🔄 📇   OK   Cancel   Help

4 Click OK to publish the synchronized files